To Nadine,

What ever road you're
on, is the right road...

Kandace Kay

LONG ROAD HOME

Kandace Kay

BALBOA
PRESS

A DIVISION OF HAY HOUSE

Balboa Press books may be ordered through booksellers or by contacting:

Balboa Press
A Division of Hay House
1663 Liberty Drive
Bloomington, IN 47403
www.balboapress.com
1-(877) 407-4847

ISBN: 978-1-4525-7700-5 (sc)
ISBN: 978-1-4525-7702-9 (hc)
ISBN: 978-1-4525-7701-2 (e)

Library of Congress Control Number: 2013911392

Printed in the United States of America.

Balboa Press rev. date: 07/23/2013

INTRODUCTION

The following passage was found in Mark's briefcase in April 2008:

Decide to be happy today, to live with what is yours: your family, your job, your luck. If you can't have what you want, maybe you can like what you have.

Just for today, be kind, cheerful, agreeable, responsive, caring, and understanding. Be your best, dress your best, talk softly, look for the bright side of things. Praise people for what they do and don't criticize them for what they cannot do. If someone does something stupid, forgive and forget. After all, it's just for one day. Who knows—it might turn out to be a nice day.

As I look outside at the red and gold leaves that dot the lawn, I know Mark would have loved this day. It saddens me to think he'll never see another day like it, but I'm tired of the sadness and want to be rid of it. Sometimes I feel I can smile. At other times the melancholy clings to me like a second skin.

Mark loved to wear a business suit. He loved the way it made him feel. He was always either in a suit or jeans—nothing in between. For my part I loved the way he smelled. He wore Stetson or Brut cologne in his early days and then Jean Paul Gaultier from Paris later on. To this day I can smell his spirit whenever he's near. A good athlete, strong and agile, he played and partied hard. He stood five feet ten inches tall, but he always struggled to put on weight, topping the scales at 148 pounds on a good day. Though not exceptionally attractive, he was a nice-looking man. He had brown hair and boasted a huge smile and a contagious belly laugh.

Toward the end of his life he didn't smile or laugh much. In fact, he struggled throughout his life with depression. But even as the darkness gripped him, I never let go of hope. I forced myself to believe tomorrow would be better. Maybe I was deluding myself. Mark, though, never had much hope. Occasionally he let us think he did, but he never fooled himself. He coped by moving our family every few years. He seemed to think the next place would provide the magic cure and take away all the darkness and depression. None of them ever did. How could they? He was running away from himself.

When I think about sharing this story, something so personal to me, something that is a part of my heart and soul, I'm more uncomfortable than I ever thought I could be. Maybe it's because once I let go of it, it won't be a piece of me anymore, and I'll have to move forward with my life—something I've been unable to do.

This is a story about life after death. It's a story about what we learn from those who have crossed over. The knowledge that they are still with us can help us heal. After the death of a loved one, someone you are so connected to, it seems impossible to survive, much less heal. Yet I did both. I learned to listen to my inner voice again, to pay attention to the signs, to trust my gut. With the help of the many people who touched my life, I was able to find the one person I thought had lost forever—me. I learned that something tragic can ultimately save you.

This is also a story about depression, addiction, and despair. It's a story about how we unintentionally let bad things into our lives and allow them to take over. Knowing they exist actually gives us power over them. My sincerest wish is for this story to touch people in a special way, to show them the light when there is nothing but darkness, to give them hope and faith that tragedy doesn't have to be tragic at all.

Chapter 1

I was almost twenty years old when I met Mark. It was September of 1977, and I was beginning my junior year at the University of Vermont (UVM), where I was a double major in physical education and psychology, with a minor in coaching. Located in northern Vermont, UVM was one of the largest colleges in the state. The Winooski River ran through its gorgeous, tree-filled campus. Snow fell in abundance in the winters, and summers were beautiful. While I was still in high school, I had spent summers on campus attending gymnastic camps. I had fallen in love with the school and its gymnastics coach. Even as a high school kid, I had known I would go to college there someday.

I had grown up in West Castleton, Vermont, a small town of about ten thousand people in the southwestern part of the state. I was the youngest of eight children, although I shared that distinction with my twin brother, Keith. Four boys, four girls. My parents divorced when I was seven because of my father's alcoholism. He died a year later, so I spent most of my childhood without a dad.

Mark was twenty when I met him, a history major from Burlington who like his father before him was destined to go on to a career in sales. He had transferred from Ithaca College in New York that fall to play hockey. We met one afternoon when my house of nine girls (six of us being college gymnasts) were getting ready to throw a birthday party for my roommates, whose birthdays were near. There was a huge cake on the table, and Mark thought it would be funny to stick his finger in it and taste the frosting. I was not impressed. I thought he was a jerk. He came to the birthday party that night, and the front porch collapsed when we stuffed it with too many students. Mark made up for his lousy first impression by showing up the next day to help fix it.

From that moment on we were friends. I saw him often, since the hockey and gymnastics teams shared the weight room. During my senior year he lived behind me just down the alley. I would watch him walk by on his way to his 8:00 a.m. class in his hiking boots, boot-cut jeans, and tan and green down jacket. I liked his look, but his body language showed a quiet struggle. He looked sad and distant, and he rarely smiled. Despite this something drew me toward him. I knew I was going to end up with him. It wasn't something I contemplated; it was something I knew like the color of my hair.

Late that winter Mark introduced me to Jack, a freshman who was also from Burlington, Vermont. I was in the commons and chatting with a friend when Mark brought him over to our table and introduced us. I stood up to chat with Jack and felt an instant connection. It was like a heat wave. He had electric blue eyes, dark hair, and a raspy voice. The way he looked deep into my dark brown eyes took my breath away and made my legs shake. Later that afternoon he looked for me on the fifth floor of the library. He wanted to see if I had felt what he had.

We enjoyed a brief but passionate affair that lasted into the summer but ended before I returned to college that fall for my teaching assignment. I don't remember how or why it ended.

Mark was still at UVM and lived nearby. We soon started jogging together. He was no longer playing hockey, and I was through with gymnastics. But we both wanted to stay in shape. We spent a lot of time together, and our friendship blossomed, slowly growing into a strong, steady relationship. Our bond was sealed one winter day when we jogged through downtown Burlington. Snow was falling, and Christmas displays twinkled in the storefront windows. I realized then we were soul mates. We were in love. It wasn't the driving, passionate kind of love I had shared with Jack; it was the kind of love that lasted forever. There was a reason we were together.

As for Jack, the passion and connection I felt with him lingered and always left me wondering. I often secretly hoped I would run into him again one day, but thirty years would pass before that wish came true.

<hr />

As the love between Mark and me thrived, I couldn't help noticing the deep sorrow that he carried with him. I remember waiting for him to smile early in our friendship. Would it be a small one just at the corners of his mouth, or would it be an eye-crinkling one? As it turned out, he had a huge, disarming smile. But he didn't unleash it often. Something haunted him.

I was also puzzled by his relationship with his family. I came from a loving family, but he wouldn't even call his parents. "Why don't you call your parents?" I would ask him. When he did call, he was always abrupt with them, like he couldn't wait to get off the phone. I sensed there was something wrong, and this little voice inside me questioned whether it was wise to become so involved with him.

I graduated with a teaching degree in December of 1979 and moved south to Montpelier, the capital of Vermont. I was ready to get out of Burlington. Mark still had a semester left at Burlington and wasn't scheduled to graduate until the following May. We made the relationship work by taking turns visiting each other. And after he graduated, we settled on Burlington as our new home. Mark really wanted to stay in his stomping grounds, and ready for a new adventure, I readily agreed. Although I moved to Burlington in the summer of 1980, I continued to job hunt in Montpelier in the hope we would eventually settle there. Unfortunately teaching jobs were as hard to find in 1980 as they are now, so after substitute teaching for a year and working odd jobs to pay the rent, I landed a sales job based out of Burlington. It was never something I wanted to do, but it was a job. My new employer was Westin Company, a fidelity and surety bonding company. I was their sales rep for three quarters of the state. I called on attorneys, bankers, and insurance agents.

Meanwhile, Mark was working as a sales rep for a transportation company. We both traveled a great deal and enjoyed meeting up on the road. But we were busy since Mark also covered the same large area of Vermont. Although his father had always pushed Mark toward a career in sales, it wasn't a natural fit. The bread and butter of a career in sales—meeting quotas, working with sales managers, and training that involved role-playing and presentations in front of people—he didn't enjoy. He hated the corporate world, responded poorly to the stressful life it entailed, and needed regular escapes to his family's lake cottage to recharge.

The cottage was located on Mirror Lake, which was about thirty-five miles north of Burlington and seven miles north of the nearest town, Birchwood. The cottage, a thousand-square-foot, three-bedroom building with an open floor plan, sat on one hundred feet of beach frontage, one of the nicest points on the lake. Stained dark blue-gray with white trim, it had a matching detached garage. Mark's parents spent—and still spend—every weekend and some of their vacations there. They had built the cottage when Mark was thirteen, and he had been retreating to its cozy confines ever since to boat, water-ski, fish, and swim in the summer and ride the snowmobile, ice fish, sled, and cross-country ski in the winter.

Mark and I started talking about getting married in early 1982 and were soon shopping for rings. We got engaged in Florida in March of that year and wanted to get married right away. But his parents convinced him we needed a long engagement and a big wedding. So after he gave me a ring, his parents monopolized the wedding plans. Where, when, how, what, why—they dictated every detail. I wanted to get married in West Castleton, but his parents refused to even attend the wedding or contribute financially if it wasn't in Burlington. I didn't fully appreciate their controlling nature until later in my marriage when it all became abundantly clear I was stuck in a toxic environment with no way out. I did wonder why (on July 19, 1983) I so desperately wanted to run out the back of the church on my wedding day. Was it just nerves or something worse?

From that day forward there was always a little voice of warning, a nagging feeling of despair. I got really good at pushing it away. I had married into this family, and I was going to make it work and create a good life. For the most part that's what we did. I really did think Mark's family just cared more than mine. I realized later they cared about the wrong thing—what a person did rather than who he or she was. My children and their relationships with their grandparents were eventually affected by this way of thinking.

James and Ruth, Mark's parents, were both born and raised in Burlington. They had lived in the same 1960s-era, split-level home since Mark's elementary school years. (They still live there today.) Along with raising Mark there, they had reared two other boys: Harry, who was two years younger than Mark and the owner of a learning disability, and Tom, who was five years younger than Mark and the youngest of the three.

James had graduated from Saint Michael's College in the Burlington area, putting himself through school, and Tom would eventually follow in his footsteps. Not Mark, though. Mark's small rebellion was all part of a larger pattern. While Tom was the good son and Harry the one with a handicap, Mark was the rebellious child. Their parents were well liked in the area, especially by the hockey community. James was your typical type-A personality: hard-charging, controlling, and manipulative. He was five feet ten, with dark hair and brown eyes. James was an athletic man and continued to play hockey and tennis well into his golden years. He retired at the age of fifty-five after a successful career as a sales manager, but he continued to tinker with his own machinery business. Mark owned his facial features, including his big smile, to his mother, Ruth, a beautiful woman with red hair and blue eyes. She never went to college, never worked as long as I knew her, and never had any interests of her own. She was a product of her husband, who controlled her every move, even finishing her sentences for her.

My life with Mark unfolded like a bad novel, one where the family was so tied together they lost their individuality. No clear lines were drawn, and once the pattern was set, no matter how hard I tried to break it, I failed. I constantly felt like a bad person for wanting things to be different, for trying to pull my family out of this environment. Deep down, I knew things were going to end badly.

Mark's family cottage at the lake became a wedge between us. For him it was a place he loved, a place he was drawn to during all his free time. If he wasn't there on the weekends and holidays, he felt like he was missing out on something. It was like a drug for him—and more important than me. His parents encouraged his addiction because it meant they never had to let go of their son. I looked at their enabling behavior like a form of brainwashing—a silent, controlling type of abuse. For me the cottage was an increasingly toxic place.

Mark rarely came to West Castleton with me because he couldn't sacrifice his cottage time. I think he was grateful when I left for weekends or occasional weekdays so he didn't have to feel badly about being there. He missed out on so many wonderful times with my family. Maybe my family was a little too real for him. Everyone was allowed their own thoughts and feelings. No one controlled anyone. There was no fear—at least not the kind that grabbed you and wouldn't let go. He also wondered at times if I would come back, knowing how I struggled. But I had made a commitment.

Like his father, Mark chose a career in sales and was convinced that this was the only avenue he could pursue successfully. His father believed that too. For example, if you chain the legs of circus elephants together and make them walk in a circle and then remove the chains, the elephants will still walk in that circle. My love for Mark was not strong enough to break the patterns long ago set by those chains. Mark would later find himself trapped in the corporate world, overwhelmed by panic. He tried to be who his father wanted him to be. Mark dreamed of being either a teacher or a chiropractor, but those dreams went unfulfilled. Never comfortable in the corporate world or in sales, he began to feel trapped.

I conceived my first baby on July 4, 1984, after I had begged Mark to stay home from the cottage for the holiday weekend. He did stay home for me but was miserable, and he made me feel terrible for asking him to sacrifice a weekend at the cottage for me. Then in October, just four months into my first pregnancy, I went into premature labor while at a high school football game. After I spent twenty-four hours in labor, I went to the hospital and had surgery to remove the fetus. I never knew the gender, only that the baby had never developed normally. Just one more sign.

After I lost the baby, I was devastated, and my grief bothered Mark's dad so much that he actually lectured me, telling me to get over it already and move on. I now realize he couldn't control how I was feeling, and that made him crazy. He was afraid when he wasn't in control because control came from fear.

I was fearful of ever trying to get pregnant again, but two years later I gave birth to my first child, a boy. We named him Charlie. It was January 30, 1986, and Mark was there for the birth at a hospital in Burlington; however, afterward he was pretty much absent. He left me alone in the hospital and then later at home all winter. I wanted to share the first weeks of our baby's life with him, but recreating became his priority. I was busy with the baby, and that gave him a reason to be absent. I accepted it because I had this wonderful, beautiful baby to care for, even though my world was less than perfect and the little voice was becoming harder and harder to ignore.

When Charlie was just three months old, we found a piece of property on the lake just down the beach from the cottage. After lengthy discussions we decided to purchase it so we could begin to pull away from the cottage time and have our own family space. This property that we would spend our summers on gave us the space I needed to survive up there.

The lake itself was beautiful. I understood why Mark was so drawn to the pristine water, the beautiful beach, and the woods. Not at all commercialized, it was a place where you could leave all your troubles behind. To this day I still love the lake but not the cottage, the lake house we eventually built on our property, or all that dwells there.

Spring brought a worsening of Mark's depression. He rarely smiled and was verbally abusive, something I wasn't going to put up with. I told him he needed to go for help—or I would take Charlie and leave. I didn't want our young son growing up in such an atmosphere. I was also confident that it would break Mark's heart to see us leave. Sure enough, he began treatment for his depression. I was hopeful he might find his way out of the darkness.

The medication helped, but things were a long way from being perfect. I wanted too much for him to feel better. Sometimes I would find myself watching him, seeing the sadness in his eyes, and I would feel helpless. I couldn't imagine going through life never feeling real joy, but that was what Mark was doing. I wanted him to find happiness and to see the future when he looked at Charlie.

Still, I figured he was making an effort and was glad for that. I stayed home with Charlie for seven months before I decided it was time to go back to work. I had quit my job with Westin Company two months before I had given birth to Charlie because my pregnancy had been considered a high-risk one and my doctor hadn't wanted me to travel anymore. Fortunately I was able to land a new job with Schmitz National Transportation Company. Although I didn't have to travel anymore, the new job, which included inside sales, entailed plenty of stress, not to mention forty-five to fifty hours a week. Every morning I dropped Charlie off with the babysitter on the way to work, and every evening I picked him up on my way home, trading my paying job for my nonpaying one.

During my first week back at work I came down with the flu. Meanwhile, Mark went out and bought a new snowmobile. There I was, sick with the flu and sadder than I thought I could ever be about leaving my baby, and all Mark could think about was his new toy. I was behaving like an adult, and all he seemed to want to do was play. The signs were getting harder to ignore.

❦

Mark's on-the-job stress continued to increase. The transportation company he worked for wasn't doing well, and the company was pushing him to transfer to Crystal Falls. He didn't want to move though, and he started hunting for a different job. Little did he know that things would remain up in the air for another two years. In the meantime he was traveling a lot for work, which put a lot of added pressure on him. When he wasn't traveling, he only wanted to be at the cottage. I think the cottage was his happy place in his head, but for me it was something much different. Whenever I walked into the place, I had a strange sense of foreboding and didn't want to be there.

Nearly two years after having Charlie, I gave birth on November 26, 1987, to our second child, a girl. Eva was stricken with pneumonia when she was just five weeks old and was hospitalized for a week as a result. With Mark snowed in at Crystal Falls, I made the decision to quit my job at Schmitz National. It was obvious he couldn't handle any responsibilities beyond his job, and I knew that I was on my own as far as parenting went. But by the time summer rolled around,

Mark had lost his job because of his refusal to move to Crystal Falls. Now we were both unemployed. How would we take care of our two small children?

I breathed a sigh of relief when Mark landed another sales job, this time in the paper industry. But as thankful as I was, I was also concerned. Mark had already struggled with so much stress and anxiety in sales. It seemed wise to consider a career that didn't involve sales. Eighteen months later when I was hired on as a sales rep for a fundraising company, I was on the job all of one month when Mark's boss told him either he had to quit his job or I had to quit mine because it was obvious he couldn't handle being a full-time employee *and* juggling parenting duties.

It was time for me to rethink *my* career. If I was going to work for a living, I realized, it would have to be in a way that didn't conflict with being a full-time parent. I eventually found a job as a part-time college recruiter. I would work nights while our babysitter, a high school student, looked after the kids. The arrangement worked well until I became pregnant with our third and final child. The pregnancy was unplanned, but when Cory was born on May 26, 1991, I decided to be a full-time, stay-at-home mom. We moved a few short weeks later, and we kept on moving once every six or seven years for the better part of the next two decades.

Of the many places we called home, one nearly brought us happiness. Later it would come to be known simply as "the big old house." Built in the early 1970s, it was a sprawling 2,400-square-foot ranch house made of brick, situated on one and a half acres. An old swimming pool sat in the backyard, which bumped up against the woods. We even had our own trail—a recreational bike trail that bisected the back woods. As for the house itself, it included four bedrooms, a big kitchen, and a family room and formal living room, which were separated by a dining room. A huge deck ran the entire length of the house and overlooked the backyard, the pool, and the woods. Two fireplaces beckoned on cold nights. A separate, heated garage gave Mark plenty of room to store and work on his toys—his boats, snowmobiles, and so on. When he wasn't at the cottage, he was in the garage, tinkering. He loved that space.

We moved to the big old house in May of 1997. Because of the age of the house and the surrounding woods, the place required regular maintenance. Mark took to joking that we didn't have four seasons there; we had *seed* seasons. Whatever tree was going to seed at the moment—birch, oak, maple—that was the season. We did a lot of raking, but we were happy.

By now Mark was working for his second paper company, and despite our cozy surroundings, he was struggling more than ever with depression. Our kids, who were all older now and developing wills and personalities of their own, were becoming harder to parent. I often felt like I was the referee, complete with black-and-white-striped jersey, between them and Mark.

One early spring day in 2003 Mark was butting heads with Eva, who was fuming because he had read her diary, and Charlie, whose car Mark had just rummaged through (and not for the first time). I had just returned from a work conference, and after I listened to everyone make their case, I took sides with the kids because I felt Mark had no respect for their privacy.

He called the kids into the kitchen and delivered a lecture I'll never forget. "A mother's love is unconditional," he told them, "but a father's love isn't. I have every right to go through your things. So long as you're living under my roof, *I'm* in control, not you."

I think he wanted to believe that controlling conditional love was the way you should parent as a father, but deep down he knew it was wrong. He would threaten the kids when he felt he had no control, leaving him feeling saddened over the realization that he was parenting his kids as his father had parented him. I always wondered if the kids understood why he sometimes acted like a crazy man toward them. At times his temper really frightened them. He became like a wild man, yelling and screaming at them sometimes for the smallest thing. I could see the fear in their eyes, and I did what I could to help them understand. I wanted them to know it was his illness and his inability to deal with stress, but all they saw was an angry, crazy man.

I wondered what it was like to grow up in his family with all the expectations and control and with no unconditional love. All children need to know their parents love them no matter what they do. Mark never had that, and I know that had an adverse effect on him. Mark did not want to parent like his parents, but he was trapped in the same patterns. His dad, who parented out of control and fear, expected his family to behave in a certain way and to always depend on him. He didn't trust that they could make decisions or figure out life without him. He truly believed that without his control everyone would fail, and he was deathly afraid of failure, even though failure was a part of life. Such an upbringing fostered anxiety and depression in Mark and robbed him of the skills necessary to survive them, and it took me years to learn that there was nothing I could do to rescue him from his past.

CHAPTER 2

Somewhere along the way I stopped listening to my inner voice and gave up on the work that might have saved my husband. We were still living in the big old house, the seventh place we had called home during our twenty-five years of married life, and despite all our problems I thought our family was the happiest it had ever been. We usually stayed in one place about six or seven years. Then my husband would get restless, and the longing to be happier and to find some phantom life that didn't exist would take over. He was "chasing happiness," as I called it, although many people can relate to such an impossible quest.

Then one beautiful fall day in 2004 I had a premonition. Some might call it a vision. It was surely a warning. The sun was shining, and the leaves on the trees were changing from green to red and gold. I was headed home, driving north on Highway 41, still in the Burlington city limits, when I went somewhere else in my mind. One moment I was seated comfortably in our four-year-old, dark gray Suburban, trying not to think about my life, and the next I was at a funeral, standing beside a wood casket with my husband's picture on it. Then I was sitting down in a church, listening to my husband's funeral. I'm not sure how long I was actually in this visionary state, but I do know that when I came out, I almost missed my exit, Birchwood Avenue, which would take me west on Highway

29 toward the lake. I was so distraught I had to pull over on the side of the road and try to shake the vision from my head. I felt like a monster for seeing such a thing. Once I regained my composure, I merged back into traffic and tucked the vision away someplace safe, someplace I thought I would never have to visit.

Mark wasn't doing well. He had switched medications again, and his job was becoming more and more uncertain because of corporate restructuring. I would listen to him throw up at night— his body's way of adjusting to yet another cocktail of medication. He lost a great deal of weight, and the stress of his inability to cope with life showed on his face.

Not long after my premonition I realized I didn't even know who I was anymore. I had become a stranger to myself. Somehow I had put myself away. The real Kandace—the fun, passionate, loving, spirited person—was replaced by someone who now lacked the skills to help anyone. Thus began a four-year-long downward spiral. The abyss had opened, and I was powerless to stop it.

The following spring in 2004 we decided to put our house up for sale. I can't even tell you why. We loved it there, and I thought we were happy. Maybe it was the spring blooms that made us feel we could have a new life too. The house was big and old. The property took a lot of maintenance, and Mark was overwhelmed with life. Once again he was looking for that place that would bring the sun back into his life. So we decided to build a house on the lake so we could return to Mark's happy place, a place that didn't exist.

Charlie, who was graduating from high school, didn't have much of a relationship with his dad, partly because Mark didn't deal with teenagers well and partly because Charlie was gay. Now things were even more stressful because Charlie wasn't sure what he wanted to do with his life after high school.

Charlie had wanted to be all grown up since he was five. The tallest of the family, he stood a thin six feet one inches tall and had ginger red hair, which was always coifed to perfection. He had his father's smile and belly laugh, and he was a cool cat just like his dad.

But he was developing an empathetic depth that Mark would never find within himself. As the firstborn son, he had a lot to live up to in the family. He had played hockey when he was younger because that was what Mark's family did, but he figured out early on that it wasn't for him. He played tennis instead and was an excellent student. His passion was—and remains—hair. He often sneaked out of the house with my hot rollers and hair products to do his friends' hair.

Mark had been the first to suspect that Charlie was gay but the last to accept it. The gay lifestyle made him uncomfortable, and he worried about Charlie's safety. How would he cope with people who didn't approve of his sexual orientation? I, too, worried about Charlie's future, but I wanted him to be true to himself. I still remember his words when he first came out.

"Mom and Dad," he told us, "being gay is only a small part of who I am. I'm still Charlie."

I always held on to that and welcomed his friends into our home. I was able to talk openly with him about his orientation, something Mark couldn't bring himself to do. Mark's parents never spoke of it, which was not surprising. They assumed he would outgrow it.

Meanwhile, Eva was a spirited teenager, always ready to challenge authority. She was also transforming into a blond bombshell before our very eyes. Her precisely highlighted locks fell onto her slender five-foot-seven frame with ease, and her eyes, small slits of turquoise, demanded a second look. She excelled at soccer and volleyball, but as the middle child, she was often overshadowed by Charlie's colorful personality and Cory's volatile nature.

At this point Cory was an athletic kid and quite skillful on the ice. Mark was his hockey coach and had been for years, although that would change once Cory entered high school. A good student with plenty of friends, Cory nevertheless struggled with anxiety and obsessive-compulsive disorder, both of which had become apparent when he was just two years old. As long as we kept him in a routine, he did fine. But when the schedule changed or when life threw the occasional curveball at him, he suffered tremendous anxiety, and rather than internalize his angst, he unleashed it in on his family, particularly me. (I eventually came to see myself as his pressure-release valve.) Often we were trying to help Mark and Cory simultaneously as father and son battled depression and anxiety respectively.

All I wanted was for everyone to be in a good place. Sometimes I wondered if that would ever happen. But by focusing so much on my family, I was losing my own identity.

We put the house on the market, and to our surprise it sold quickly. Now we had to find a builder, a house plan, and a place to live while we built—and we thought we were *reducing* our stress!

What are we doing? I kept asking myself. *Are we crazy? This is going to end badly.* Doubt nagged at me constantly. But I did nothing.

We found a big rental house—big enough for all our stuff—that was just five miles away from the house we had just sold and thus still in the same school district and close to the kids' friends. Located in the village of Hillary, a subdivision of Burlington, the house was white, with two stories and three bedrooms, and it sat on five wooded acres. It was a charming house with a large kitchen and an inviting attached sunroom, but it was quite close to the corner of Hillcrest Road and Highway 29, both busy thoroughfares. (Highway 29 led west to the lake.) It had two important features going for it in any case. It was only forty minutes from the lake, and it had a big detached garage where we could store all our things.

Since Mark was too busy with work to really help, the move, which was already extremely stressful, became my job. I embraced it like I did all challenges, but I became increasingly depressed at the same time. It felt like I was shouldering the entire burden of our lives. I was unwise, I now realize, to ignore my inner voice, which kept telling me we were on the wrong path.

After we settled in, we shifted our focus to Cory's anxiety and anger. We didn't want to put him on medication, so we went the behavior modification route. Eva didn't spend much time at home because it was a stressful and unhappy place. Charlie had moved out after graduation and had found a one-bedroom apartment on Burlington's west side, where he would stay for less than a year. As for Mark, his depression and anxiety had worsened with the increasing uncertainty about his job and the stress of building the house.

Nevertheless, we continued to move forward with the building throughout the summer and visited the building site often. The site was a quarter mile down the road from Mark's parents' cottage and sat on a wooded lot with one hundred feet of beach frontage. It was one of the nicest lots on the lake. We had owned it since 1987 and had spent many glorious summers camping there. Thus, there was already a well onsite, plus a septic system. Eva, who often had to stay at the rental house because of her job, began to feel left out of the building process. I wasn't being much of a mother to her, but between worrying about Mark and trying to help Cory, I was spread too thin. How had our lives gotten so out of control? And why couldn't I do something about it? Where had Kandace gone? How was she going to find her way back?

Then one day my husband was working in his office at the rental house when he lost it. He had been trying to deal with his job and the fact that his company was restructuring, but his coping skills were pretty much nonexistent. After a conversation with his boss he hung up the phone, flew out the front door, and didn't stop until he had reached the high retaining wall that overlooked Hillcrest Road, where he proceeded to scream and pace.

As I watched from the front lawn, I felt like I was watching our lives scatter to the wind. Although I knew he was teetering on that wall and might jump at any second, I didn't know what to say or how to help. So I did nothing but watch—watch him struggle with work, life, and the choices we had made. We actually talked about pulling the lake house project that night and drove around the neighborhoods, looking for houses for sale, but we decided it was too late to turn back and too late to change our minds. This was my opportunity to take the reins. But I froze. I knew this was an unhealthy man and a very unhealthy situation we had created, but I didn't know what to do about it. I felt paralyzed, unable to help anyone, even myself.

Our plan was to stay in the rental until the lake house was finished, but the owners of the rental decided in November to move back to the area (and back into their house). Since we had a month-to-month lease, we had to get out by the end of the month. We didn't have a lot of options because we only needed to stay somewhere for about three months. So we ended up moving into the cottage, just down the road from the lake house, and putting our things in the garage of the new house. My inner voice was growing louder . . . and more difficult to ignore. The realization that this was my life now finally sank in when I drove up to the lake after work for the first time. Suddenly overcome by a wave of nausea, I thought I was going to have to pull over and get sick on the side of the road. I was behaving in ways I knew were wrong and could even harm us. What had I let happen?

CHAPTER 3

We lived in the cottage a little over three months until the lake house was ready, and during that time we weathered a typical Vermont winter at Mirror Lake. The lake was frozen by Thanksgiving, and soon afterward we were enjoying huge pickup hockey games out on the ice or ice skating from lake to lake. By Christmas the lake and its environs were buried in close to a foot of snow. The snow would continue to fall until mid-March, and the mercury would dip as low as twenty degrees below Fahrenheit on some days and climb as high as a balmy thirty degrees—considered warm by hardy locals—on others.

Adjusting to the commute in the winter was a challenge in itself. I constantly worried about the kids' commute to school (thirty-five minutes one way), my commute to work (forty-five minutes one way) and Mark's adjustment to working in a small, inadequate home office. His frustration with his job grew deeper, and now that we were at the lake, his outlet was to recreate. Often I would come home from work and find that he was not working at all but playing on the lake, where he could escape his demons.

Meanwhile, Cory's behavior was growing increasingly worse. He did not do well with change, and the two moves in six months were catastrophic. His rage was out of control. He actually kicked in the side of the kitchen cabinet one night and threatened us. We had to call the police to intervene. Why was I so paralyzed? It was almost as if we weren't in control anymore, as if an outside force were controlling us.

As the lake house took shape, I got excited about the prospect of living in a new house, one that overlooked the most beautiful lake imaginable. The place was almost magical, and the excitement allowed me to ignore my inner voice at times. But when I would walk over to the house to visit with the builder or check the progress, I would sit in a sunny spot in the snow outside the front of the house and cry. It was almost as if something or someone else was controlling my emotions. Why was I so sad?

With its green siding and white trim, the three-story, four-bedroom lake house was nothing short of striking. A great room, bedroom, bathroom, and storage occupied the lower level. Another great room, a master bedroom and bathroom, the kitchen, and Mark's office took up the main floor. And two bedrooms with dormers constituted the top floor. Two wood-burning fireplaces were capable of heating the entire house. From the huge screened porch overlooking the lake, you could look down at our own sandy beach plus our dock, which was complete with lifts for the boat and Jet Ski. But the lake house's main feature was light. Built for Mark's depression, it was riddled with windows to let in ample sunlight. The woodwork, painted white, filled the house with reflected light. And every lake-facing window offered breathtaking views of the water. Eagles soared by the oversized windows every day. How was it not possible to be happy here? Hadn't this been our dream ever since we had bought the lake property?

We moved into the lake house mid-March 2006. I remember the day, which was busy, hectic, and totally overwhelming. I had my first ever panic attack while I was standing in the kitchen. As I grew dizzy and began to sweat, shake, and feel sick to my stomach, I realized that this was not where we belonged. Something terrible was connected to this place. I couldn't breathe. I had to run outside and get some air. I breathed in deeply, hoping to feel renewed, but nothing could shake the truth.

Mark loved his new home office, which was full of light, but he still found it difficult to concentrate. Instead of dealing with his job or his boss, he would go outside and play—skating, ice fishing, or riding the snowmobile. That concerned me a little, but I figured if he was able to relax and be happy, this meant he was doing better.

We made it through the summer, and in August we took Eva to college. Like her mother and father before her, she would be attending the University of Vermont. Her plan was to major in political science and minor in information systems. She wanted to become a lawyer. Meanwhile, Charlie was attending Aveda Institute, a beauty school. After he had moved three times in less than three years, he had finally settled in Minneapolis, where he was living with two roommates on the top floor of an old building downtown and paying the bills by working shifts at a trendy clothing store.

After Eva left, it was just the three of us—Cory, my husband, and I—at the lake house. Cory was a difficult kid to raise since he and his father had similar issues, and Mark didn't always deal very well with him. I was trying my best to be there for both of them, especially Cory. But despite the turmoil, father and son became best buddies. Mark loved his toys—his boat and his snowmobile—and the two spent hours recreating together on the lake. While they grew closer, my relationship with Mark became more strained. We weren't as close as we had been in the past. In fact, we were growing apart.

Meanwhile, Mark's company wasn't doing well and was in the midst of reorganizing. Would they let Mark go during the reorganization? It seemed likely. Mark's knowledge of this fact sent him over the edge, and his depression took a darker turn. He was different. The pain had become who he was. I began to suspect he was in a place where he was capable of hurting himself.

We worked hard that summer and early fall building a retaining wall made of field stones, the three of us doing all the work ourselves. But the wall, along with Mark's recreational activities, took him away from his work. By October Mark was suffering from a sports hernia. Was it the wall or all the recreating? He decided to have surgery.

I was sitting by his bedside at the hospital in Montpelier when the nurse arrived to wheel him to the operating room. I gave him a hug and a kiss.

"If I don't wake up," he said after he pulled me close, "it's because I don't want to."

This was a warning sign, a quiet call for help.

He recovered in a couple weeks, but the pain really didn't go away. He became increasingly depressed.

Later that month on Halloween Cory was playing in his last preseason hockey game when a player checked him from behind with his elbow and shattered his collarbone, breaking it into three pieces. It was a very bad break. Cory spent two days at a medical center in Burlington. Mark still wasn't quite recovered from his surgery, and now we were dealing with Cory, whose injury would keep him off the ice during his freshman year of hockey. Surgeons inserted a plate and nine screws to repair Cory's shattered collarbone.

How am I going to do this? I asked myself more than once. Mark and Cory were both in pain, both in a dark place. I was surrounded by sadness. All my instincts were telling me that as long as we lived at the lake, nothing good was going to happen. But I did nothing, said nothing.

Cory missed a week of school and was anxious about going back in pain and in a sling. It was tough enough being a freshman at a new school, but to be taken out of your sport and have to manage with one arm made it much worse. Mark was rehabbing his way back from his surgery and was behind in work. Worse, his boss was ignoring him, which caused him to believe things were going to come to a head with the reorganization. His anxiety and depression were off the charts. Even the medication he was on wasn't making a difference.

In early November Mark pulled into the parking lot where I worked and called me at my desk. I was a volunteer manager and helped run the at-risk swim program at a local recreational center where I had worked for the last ten years.

"I'm in trouble," he said in a tone that wasn't so much hysterical as it was resigned. He sounded deeply sad. "I need your help. Please come out here right now."

I dropped everything and ran out to the car, leaving my coworkers to wonder what was going on. It was sunny outside, and the air was mild—mild enough that I only needed a light sweater. I opened the door to his shiny, new white Chevy Grand Prix, one of many company cars he'd had throughout his sales career, and found him sitting behind the wheel. Dressed to a T in a crisp white shirt, bright yellow tie, black dress slacks, and perfectly shined Allen Edmonds dress shoes, he had his head down in utter resignation and his hands on the wheel.

I wanted to cry. I wanted to scream at him and tell him, "I can't do this anymore!" Instead, I calmly sat down next to him.

"I'm going to hurt myself," he said as soon as I closed the door. "I'm in a bad place, and I don't know what to do."

So I took charge. I told him he needed to take some time off from work to get his depression under control and that it was a good way to buy him some time and let this reorganization shake out while he was under some medical care. Next I called his doctor and the human resources department at his company and got the ball rolling for twelve weeks off under the Family and Medical Leave Act. We did this while we sat in the car. I then had him drive right to his psychiatrist's office for immediate help. Admittedly I was skeptical of his psychiatrist, who I thought was too easily manipulated. Indeed, Mark could dictate what medications he wanted and then would play with the doses. I often heard him in the bathroom cutting his pills, and if I said something, he would holler back, "Mind your own business!" He called himself his own pharmacist.

During his twelve weeks off Mark became obsessed with finding another job. Instead of just relaxing, healing, and managing his depression, he fueled the problem.

"I want to show you something," he said one day after I got home from work. He was dressed in a pair of jeans and an old hockey sweatshirt and had been puttering in the garage.

"Okay," I replied.

We walked out into the garage, and there on the floor was a pile of shiny drier pipes, cardboard, and tape.

"What's this?" I asked.

"It's my suicide kit," he answered matter-of-factly.

I froze with fear. *How should I react?* I didn't want to act alarmed or scold him, so I calmly replied, "You're going to get rid of this stuff, right?"

"Of course." His voice was robotic, emotionless. "I'm so much better now."

I went back into the house, sat down on the kitchen floor behind the kitchen island, and cried. I felt completely hopeless. The pile disappeared, and we never talked about it again. My fear however remained.

⸻

After the holidays Mark learned of a sales job that had just opened up at a manufacturing company in the paper industry, one that Mark thought was doing better than his own. He promptly applied for the position, but I told him that perhaps he should consider something entirely different, something that would make him happy, even if it meant selling the lake house and moving. I thought it would be an adventure. Mark thought it would be a failure. When his twelve weeks off were up and he returned to his job, he was immediately let go. All his fears were validated, but he was relieved to have another sales job waiting in the wings. He was scheduled to start work in early February of 2007 and would train at the company's home office in Hartsville, South Carolina, after which time he would cover sales in the local area, including Burlington and Richmond. I was concerned. This was not a healthy man, and now he was taking on the stress of a new job.

The week before he was slated to start his new job, Eva was still home on Christmas break, and Cory was starting to practice hockey again. The air was cold, and the snow had settled in for the winter, leaving a blanket of white everywhere. I thought things were looking a little brighter. Maybe we had weathered the storm. Cory and Mark had gone into Burlington on a Sunday night so Mark could play Sunday night hockey and Cory could stay at his grandparents' house and get up early the next morning for hockey practice.

Sunday night as the snow came down hard, Mark decided to stay after hockey and drink beer with the boys. He often did this, not to my liking because it was always too much and too late. He had purchased a 2004 Toyota Celica—decked out with after-market parts like a spoiler, wheel covers, and tinted windows—for Cory to drive to school as soon as he got his license, and he wanted to see how that baby handled in the snow. So he ripped around on the snowy roads. He was having fun. It was late, and he didn't think too much about it until he saw the flashing lights behind him. He didn't know how long they had been there, but he certainly knew it was not good. He was immediately pulled from the car and handcuffed and then cited for fleeing an officer, driving under the influence, and reckless driving. He was thrown into jail, and his car had to be towed. He didn't make it to his parents' house, where a worried Cory was waiting for him.

The consequences of his joyride were going to be astronomical—hiring an attorney, paying for the citations, and absorbing higher insurance premiums. But what would happen with his new job? Would he be fired before he even worked one day? I was furious. I didn't cut him any slack either. How could he have been so reckless? Weren't things just starting to look up for him? The nagging voice

I had gotten so good at ignoring started pounding in my ears. I felt like we were spinning out of control.

When he told his company about his tickets and the charges, he was immediately put on probation and required to attend a hearing. Although the punishment was a mere hand slapping by a bunch of corporate types, it was nevertheless humiliating for Mark. The onus was on him to prove that this behavior wasn't the norm for him and that he wasn't reckless.

Living with the OWI (operating while intoxicated) was difficult, but we managed to get past it for the most part. Mark's parents insisted on helping Mark with the attorney fees, and Mark let them. I thought it was a bad idea. I didn't want to let them get involved and thought it would come back to haunt Mark.

"I'll never live to be an old man," Mark said to me more than once. "You'll go back. You'll move back to southern Vermont, right?"

"What are you talking about?" I would ask him.

Even when we were helping out with a hockey fundraiser, there were comments from the alumni we contacted. People had heard about his OWI.

Mark and I were the chairs, and we had to contact an old boyfriend of mine whose name was on the mailing list because he had gone to the same high school.

"You should have married him," Mark said. "He would have been a better choice."

"What are you talking about?" I asked.

"Well, don't you ever wonder about what he's doing or what it would have been like?"

"Stop it," I said. "Just stop it."

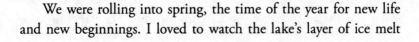

We were rolling into spring, the time of the year for new life and new beginnings. I loved to watch the lake's layer of ice melt away to reveal crystal-clear water. Wildlife, too, would return to the lake. I would watch the loons fly in to mate sometimes before all the ice was gone. The fish would arrive to spawn, digging their nests in the sand. I could lay on the dock for hours just watching the lake come to life. I especially enjoyed wrapping myself in a blanket, walking down to the beach in the early morning, and watching the sunrise. The lake was a place where I could escape my worries and the darkness engulfing me, a place where I could recharge so I could get through another day, a place where I could silence the voice and tame the tummy.

Mark's depression was deepening. It had now become who he was. It surrounded him and took on a life of its own. He could still get through his days. He could still function. But he wasn't Mark. He had a look in his eyes I didn't recognize. I sensed he wasn't quite there with us all the time. Nevertheless, we managed to get through the second summer on the lake. The kids did their best to find jobs, and we spent a lot of time on the water, enjoying the lake. I would have to say that the summer of 2007 was fun. I didn't work a lot in the summer, so I could be there to enjoy it when the kids were around and spend my quiet time there as well.

I began to swim again, logging many miles that summer in hopes of eventually joining a masters' swim club. Swimming took me back to my roots. I had first swum competitively at the tender age of eight and had continued to compete all the way through high school. During my college years I had even trained as a lifeguard. Now so many years later I still loved to swim and teach swimming.

After Eva went back to school in the fall and after Cory and I returned to our respective routines of commuting to school and work, I decided to get lifeguard certified to help with the running of my at-risk swim program at the recreational center. The program, which taught water safety to second and third graders, was aimed toward at-risk schools, schools where 70percent or more of the students were living at or below the poverty line. It ran only during the school year, which meant my summers were light but the rest of the year was fairly busy. I was passionate about the program—always motivated, always happy to be involved. I was that bright light everyone was attracted to. In short, I loved my work. But when I started working more, Mark voiced his disapproval. He wasn't a fan of the longer hours because they took time away from the family and didn't make us much money. For me it wasn't about the money; it was about the passion, about doing something I cared deeply about. But no matter what I did outside the house, I was always pulled back in because of the neediness, darkness, depression, and despair. I was now fighting for my life. I was desperate to find myself again, to live outside the illness and what it did to my family.

Mark spent more and more time recreating with Cory. That was their outlet, and I felt left out. I was spending much of my time alone at the lake house. When winter came, I was pretty much deserted. If I said anything to Mark about it, he would get angry and put me down, telling me I didn't have any interests and that I never wanted to do anything. Because, you see, if it wasn't what Mark wanted to do, it was nothing. He needed the feeling he got from riding the snowmobile. It was like a drug. And when I threatened it, he fought back.

I became quiet and withdrawn. I didn't like how I felt, how off everything was, how Mark's priorities were all messed up, how the only time he was happy was when he was on his snowmobile or in his boat. I couldn't help anymore. I wasn't enough. I couldn't find myself. I was lost and living in a place that was toxic.

I see things more clearly now. I think he was trying to separate himself from me, to find reasons to put some distance between us. Were we living at the lake or drowning in it?

I should have known something was seriously wrong one Saturday in early April when Mark dropped me off at the pool. While I swam laps, he ran errands. Afterward I was just exiting the locker room when he showed up, clearly disappointed that he hadn't returned in time to watch me swim laps. *He can always catch me next time*, I thought, but he seemed crestfallen. I was touched that he had wanted to watch me, but the nagging voice in the back of my head was now in full-on alarm mode. Why did he suddenly appreciate how much I loved to swim and how happy I was in the water? Why now?

CHAPTER 4

Spring was my time. I always felt renewed—like anything was possible. I could get away to do and be whatever I chose to do or be. The feeling of freedom exhilarated me. But the weather so far in the spring of 2008 had been awful. We were several days into April, and so far all we had experienced was sleet, rain, and wind. I needed a break. I was therefore looking forward to the three-day weekend ahead. Eva and I were planning to meet in Montpelier and continue down to my sister's dairy farm in southern Vermont for some much needed relaxation as well as some mother-daughter bonding.

Cory was already in Burlington, where he was staying at his aunt and uncle's house and looking after their dog while they vacationed in Florida. Sue and Tom had never had any children, and Rory, their springer spaniel, was their baby.

Meanwhile, Mark was in Manchester on business. He wasn't due back from his trip until late Thursday night or early Friday morning, but because of the weather, I asked him to consider coming home earlier on Thursday so I could use his company car for the trip to my sister's farm. The car, a big, brand-new Chevy Impala, was better in snow than my wine red 1985 Dodge Conquest, a two-door hatchback that sat low on the pavement and was treaded with racing tires. We typically left the Conquest in the garage during the winter as it was fast-approaching collector-car status. Mark wasn't done with his business trip, but I pushed . . . really hard. I was grasping at anything that would make me feel better and take me away from the lake house. I talked him into coming home early, even though he knew he still had obligations in Manchester.

I left home extremely early on Thursday morning to give a presentation at work. I had already made arrangements to meet Mark later that afternoon at a gas station to switch cars. As luck would have it, when three o'clock rolled around, I pulled into the gas station on Oneida Street in Burlington just as Mark was arriving in the Impala. He pulled up to the nearest pump so he could fill the Impala's gas tank for me, and I watched gratefully as he stood outside and pumped gas in the horizontal sleet. Fortunately, he was wearing a blue and black Columbia ski jacket, which helped him weather the elements.

As soon as he had finished, we sat in my Conquest and chatted for a few minutes. He seemed distant, slightly down, like he was struggling again. His body language was that of a defeated man.

"Thank you again for making this trip happen for me," I said. "I really need to get away."

I asked him what he had planned for the evening, and he told me he was going to go with his good friend Aaron among others to a snowmobile show at the Expo Center. I knew that meant he and his buddies would be barhopping afterward. I reminded him about our dog, who'd been locked inside since 6:00 a.m., when I'd left for work, and told him not to stay out too late. The drive home would take him a solid forty-five minutes on a good night. The snow and sleet would add at least fifteen minutes.

We talked a bit and then got out of the car together. I grabbed my overnight bag and tossed it into the Impala. I then pulled him close, and taking hold of the collar of his ski jacket, I gave him a kiss.

"I love you," I said. "Please don't stay out too late. And don't drink too much."

As I jumped into the driver's seat, Mark leaned in and grabbed the garage door opener.

"Why are you taking that?" I asked.

"I don't have one," he answered.

"Yes, you do. There's one in the Conquest."

He took it anyway.

Eva and I arrived that evening at Lizzy's farm. My second oldest sibling and a born caretaker, Lizzy had always been like my second mom. She stood a lean five feet nine inches tall, with dark hair, dark brown eyes, and a take-charge personality that always made those around her feel safe and protected. Her dairy farm, which was located high in the rolling hills of Rutland County in southern Vermont, was home to two hundred head of cattle—dairy, beef, and young stock. Acres and acres of crops surrounded a hundred-year-old farmhouse, which sat on top of a hill and offered a spectacular view of the surrounding countryside. Inside the old white farmhouse were five bedrooms, hardwood floors, oversized windows, and a huge dining room with a table big enough to host the whole family and then some. Lizzy's old farmhouse wrapped itself around you like your mother's homemade quilt, leaving you feeling safe and warm.

The next day, Friday, we had only been up a few hours when Mark called me. I could tell he was upset.

"What's wrong?"

"Nothing," he said. "Just a problem with one of my accounts at work, and I'm stressed. How are things going at the farm?"

"Fine," I lied.

In truth, Eva and I had been fighting about her on-again-off-again boyfriend, whom Mark didn't like. But I didn't dare mention it. I knew it would upset Mark. I told him I had to go and I would call him back in the morning.

When Saturday morning rolled around, I didn't bother to call. I needed a break, and things were still dicey with Eva.

So *he* called *me*.

"Why didn't you call?" he asked angrily.

I finally mentioned the dust-up with Eva, but I kept it brief and tried to make light of it. "We're going into West Castleton to see my mom," I said. "What are you doing?"

"Working," he answered. "I'll talk to you later."

We hung up.

Then Eva came downstairs. "Why did Dad try to call me?" she asked.

"I'm not sure," I said. "I just talked to him, and he seems really stressed."

"I won't call him back then," she said.

Eva and I decided to agree to disagree about our argument and have a nice weekend despite our spat. The depression and anger around us was threatening to devour us, and we didn't need more.

The following morning, Sunday, we were up early so we would have time to stop in Montpelier for some shopping before we headed home to the lake house.

Eva came downstairs with a concerned expression on her face. "Dad called me and apologized for being so hard on me. He also told me that he loved me very much." She locked eyes with me. "Do you think he's all right?"

"I think so. He just sounds really sad and stressed." I knew he was struggling lately, but I wasn't alarmed.

Mark called me just as we were ready to get in the car to leave the farm. "When are you coming home?" he asked.

"Sooner rather than later," I answered.

"What's the hurry?" he asked.

"What do you mean, 'What's the hurry?'" I asked.

"I just mean there's no rush," he said. He sounded like he'd been crying.

"I know. I'm just ready to come home. Are you okay?"

"Yes," he said.

"But you sound like you've been crying. Are you sure you're okay?"

"I'm fine. Just getting a cold."

I was mildly concerned now.

Before we hung up, he said, "Don't forget how much I love you."

"Well, yeah," I replied, "I love you too."

Eva and I got into the car and headed to Montpelier to shop a little, have lunch with my sister-in-law, and then drive back to the lake.

While we were shopping, I noticed Eva kept walking away from me and texting and talking on her cell. She was so distracted, and I was getting a little annoyed.

We arrived home at about 4:30 p.m. to find Cory lying on the couch, watching television.

"Where's Dad?" Eva asked.

"He wasn't home when I got here," Cory said in a concerned tone. "But there's a hole in the garage wall where he backed the boat up."

"What's going on?" I asked suspiciously.

Eva and Cory traded glances.

"We think Dad might be suicidal," Eva said.

"Why?" I asked in alarm.

"Well," Eva answered, "Dad called Cory and told him that if he wasn't home, it was 'cause he'd gone for a drive."

Mark never talked like that. He never just "went for a drive."

"What else?" I asked.

"I called Charlie and asked if Dad had called him," Eva said, "and he said yes but he didn't pick up and hadn't listened to the voice mail yet. I told him to listen to it and call me back. That was when I called Cory back and told him to go home, drop off the dog at Grandpa and Grandma's house, and get here as quickly as possible. Right after that Charlie called me back and said Dad apologized on his voice mail for not being there for him and told him how much he loved him. Charlie's still not convinced Dad's going to hurt himself, but Cory and I are."

"Why didn't you tell me this sooner?" I asked.

"We didn't want to worry you," Eva answered.

I made dinner, but few words were spoken around the table. By now each of us was weighed down by fear, but no one wanted to give voice to that fear or believe the worst. So we made small talk. Eva talked about going back to school the next morning. Had Mark gassed up her car and checked her oil like he usually did? I asked Cory if he had any homework to finish and whether or not he had a track meet scheduled for the week. For my part I was due in Burlington at 7:45 the next morning. Monday was my day to pull lifeguard duty at the downtown rec center pool.

After dinner I left the first of many messages on Mark's cell. "Dinner's ready," I said. "Where are you? Are you coming home? Call me back!"

CHAPTER 5

By 7:30 that night I was getting really worried. I decided to call Aaron to see if he had any idea where Mark was. I reached his wife, who suggested I call his cell phone because he was up at their cottage, working on the roof.

"Have you seen Mark?" I asked him as soon as he picked up. "He hasn't come home, and we're starting to get worried."

"I haven't seen or talked to him," he answered. "But don't worry. He's probably just looking at cars or boats somewhere."

I was standing in front of the kitchen window and staring out at the lake when I hung up with Aaron. I started thinking about Mark's triggers. If he was suicidal, it was because he had gotten another OWI or had been fired from his job. I called the kids into the kitchen.

"Something must have happened," I told Eva and Cory. "Your dad wouldn't just not come home. Let's start looking around the house for clues. Cory, you go downstairs. Check the great room, back room, and the work area. Eva, look around his office—in his desk drawers and through the notes on his desk. I'll check the bedroom and make sure his suitcase, clothes, and shaving kit are still there. I'll also make sure the gun is still secure."

Suddenly we had a purpose—to search for clues—and the atmosphere became more electrically charged as a result. While the kids went off to begin their respective investigations, I looked in our walk-in closet and found that no overnight bags were missing. Next I checked to see if the gun was still in its safe place with the safety on—it was. I then looked for his shaving kit in our bathroom. It was there in the drawer, but all his medication was gone. Mark usually had three or four prescription bottles at any time, and they were all gone. All of them.

I ran into the great room and gathered the kids. "Your dad's meds are all missing," I said. "I'm calling the police and filing a missing person's report with a suicide alert."

I dialed 911 and felt instant relief. It felt good to at least be doing something, to be putting a plan in place.

While we waited for the police to arrive, Eva reported that Mark's desk was covered with paperwork. It looked as if he'd just gotten up and left without finishing his work. The work room, too, was quite a mess, according to Cory. There were metal shavings all over the floor near the tool bench.

The police arrived within ten minutes. We were pretty good friends with the police up there because it was such a remote area. They watched out for us. We sat around the kitchen table, filed the report, and also answered their many questions: "When was the last time you saw or spoke to your husband? What were your conversations with him like? Did anything happen in the last few days that would trigger suicidal behavior? What makes you think he would hurt himself? Has he ever been missing before? Has he ever been suicidal before? Does he take medication for his depression? Is he under a doctor's care? What are some places he would go, his hangouts? Does he consume alcohol? Would he be in a bar somewhere? How well does he know the woods and area up here? What car was he driving? What was he wearing?"

We gave the officers Mark's cell phone company information so they could try to track it. At this point we still didn't know if anything had happened to trigger a suicide attempt, but we knew enough to know it was possible that Mark had done something terrible.

I noticed Mark had not checked the oil or gassed up Eva's car for her return trip to school, so Eva and I decided to take care of it. Before we went to the gas station, we drove down the cottage driveway to have a look around. Maybe we would see something or find a clue. I knew we couldn't get into the garage because the last ice storm had knocked the power out and the electric garage door opener didn't work. I didn't have a key on me for the service door, so we just walked the outside perimeter. Eva was noticeably spooked.

"Let's go," she said nervously. She couldn't explain why, but she wanted out of there.

We left without checking to see if the cottage was locked or unlocked. But nothing appeared out of place. Earlier I had told the police when they had asked about the cottage that we couldn't get in because the power was out, so they hadn't tried to get in either.

Once we got back from servicing Eva's car, we settled into the great room and turned on the television. We could hear Cory upstairs in his room also watching TV.

Eva had barely gotten comfortable on the love seat in front of the big windows overlooking the lake when she got up suddenly. "I can't sit here in front of these windows," she said. "It's scaring me."

She moved to Mark's chair, an oversized La-Z-Boy recliner. Dark gold and upholstered in a rough corduroy type of fabric, it rocked unless it was in a reclining position. She sat there for maybe a minute and then jumped up.

"I can't sit here either. I'm getting the weirdest feelings. I feel a strange energy here in this chair."

She finally settled in next to me on the couch, where we cuddled together and tried to watch TV.

I kept getting up every fifteen minutes to check the garage, certain I'd just heard the garage door go up. But each time I opened the door in the kitchen that led to the garage, I found it empty. The unspoken realization—that Mark had taken his own life—hung in the air like a thick fog. My stomach was in knots. I felt utterly hopeless.

I finally went to the master bedroom, which was right off the great room, and lay on top of the comforter on Mark's side. Too tired to undress, I clutched at his pillow, praying we would find him alive.

Eva, not wanting to be left alone, decided to go upstairs to her room. When she caught a glimpse of me lying on Mark's side of the bed, she lost it. She ran upstairs and crawled into bed with Cory, sobbing.

None of us got any sleep that night. By six o'clock the next morning we were all up, showered, and ready to try to find Mark. I left a message at work that I would not be in and that I was in the middle of a family crisis. We stopped by the police station to check on any progress they might have made in the night but learned nothing. They hadn't even received any cooperation from the cell phone company, just a request to call back in the morning.

I informed the policewoman that we were going into Burlington to check hospitals and visit Mark's doctor. She said she would notify the officers in charge.

We drove to all three hospitals in the area and asked around at all the emergency rooms. We checked the hockey rinks. At his doctor's office we left a note with the receptionist that we had to speak with Dr. Smith immediately. It was urgent. Then we waited. The waiting was torturous. With no sleep and the stress of Mark missing, I became punchy. We were sitting off to the side in the waiting room when one of the guys that Mark played hockey with on Sunday nights entered. I was so nervous about having to explain why we were there that I had the kids shield me from his sight, and when that failed, I ran into the ladies' room. I kept sticking my head out of the door and asking if he was still there.

"Mom," Cory said, "why are you so crazy?"

Finally we saw a patient exit out of the doctor's office, and the three of us ran down the long hallway and barged inside.

Dr. Smith's office was tastefully decorated just like the rest of the clinic—a sleek, modern building with lots of windows and exposed ceiling beams painted purple. Cherry wood shelving units ran along one wall and an assortment of art hung on the others.

Dr. Smith sat behind an intimidatingly large desk, also made of cherry wood. Handsome, five feet eight inches tall, and in his late forties or early fifties, the doctor always had a Diet Pepsi in his hand or on his desk. He looked gentle and friendly enough, but I found him defensive and abrasive. I also didn't appreciate the way he hid behind his desk, which lent him an unapproachable air. Mark had liked him because he had always been able to manipulate him and get whatever medication he wanted. It was like Mark was in charge and not Dr. Smith.

We told Dr. Smith that Mark was missing and asked if he had heard from him.

"I haven't heard from him," he said and then checked the notes from Mark's last visit the week before. "Let's see. All he talked about was you and the kids. He didn't talk about himself or how he felt at all."

Isn't that a red flag? I wondered. *Doesn't he get that?*

"I feel like Mark has been distancing himself from me the past several weeks," I said. "Have you noticed anything off with him?"

"Well, I can assure you he doesn't have enough medication on him to kill himself," Dr. Smith said.

We left his office, completely frustrated by Dr. Smith's inability and unwillingness to help us. If Mark had tried to give himself an overdose, our only hope was that he might be still alive somewhere— passed out but still alive. But where? We needed another plan.

We decided it was time to talk to Mark's parents, who had just returned from a vacation the night before. I called the house, and Mark's handicapped younger brother, Harry, answered. Harry still lived at home. He told me that their mother was out walking and that their father was on his way to visit their Uncle Peter, who had dementia. I told Harry to keep his mom home when she returned, and then I proceeded to call Uncle Peter. Trying to communicate with him was impossible. He had no idea who I was or what I was talking about. He didn't even know that Mark's father was coming. I was shouting into the phone as if he were hard of hearing and not just confused. The kids began to laugh, and I began to laugh. And we all broke down into hysterics.

We finally managed to get everyone to meet at Mark's parents' house at 11:00 a.m. The kids and I were starving, so we stopped off at a bakery to grab some muffins and juice. When we arrived at the house, Mark's mom, dad, and Uncle Carl, a retired police detective from Florida, were there.

"What's going on?" they asked.

"Mark is missing," I said, "and we're worried. We think he's suicidal."

"No, he's not," Mark's dad said. "He probably just lost track of time."

"No, he's been missing all night. He never came home, and he's not answering his cell phone."

Mark's mom kept trying to come up with ideas as to where he might be, and it was annoying. She wasn't helping. Mark's dad told me to call his brother Mitch, who was also a retired detective in Burlington, to see if there was anything I could do that I hadn't done already.

I did as he suggested. I said as soon as he answered, "Mark has been missing since yesterday morning. I think he might be suicidal."

"Oh, come on. Mark would never do something like that."

"Mitch, he suffers from depression. Something must have happened when we were out of town because he kept making good-bye phone calls to all of us. When we got home, he wasn't there." I told Mitch everything I had done so far—filing the missing person report, checking all the hospitals and his hangout spots, talking to his doctor, and calling his friends.

"You did all the right things," he said. "Now let the police do their work."

We hung up.

Only the kids and I really knew how Mark suffered with this illness. Only we knew what he might be capable of if things got too tough, although we still had no idea what could have happened to put Mark in this place.

Mark's dad was still trying to come up with ideas as to where Mark could be. "Did you check the cottage and the garage?" he asked.

"No," I said. "The power's out, and you can't get in through the big overhead door. I didn't have a key on me, so I didn't even try to get in."

"I showed Mark how to jerry-rig the door to the garage so he could get in," he said.

"You did what?" I asked.

"I showed Mark how to Jerry-rig the door to get power so he could open it if he needed to get in the garage," he answered.

Oh, my God, I thought. My heart sank. I walked outside and burst into tears. I knew right then and there where Mark was. I knew it like I knew my own name.

I numbly agreed to a plan of action. Mark's dad and his uncle would go check out the cottage. Eva and I would go home and trace credit card activity. Cory would take the four-wheeler out in the woods and check the logging roads. We all left for the lake.

CHAPTER 6

I sat down at Mark's desk and went online to check our credit card and bank accounts. There had been no activity. I could hear Cory starting up the four-wheeler when Eva came running through the front door.

"I got into Dad's voice mail!" she said excitedly. "I changed his password and got in! Something happened, Mom!" I could hear the panic in her voice. "Aaron left him all sorts of voice mails, saying he couldn't find him and that he was driving up and down Highway 29, looking for him. Then he called him yesterday and told him to go home and tell us what had happened, that it would be okay."

As I sat there listening to Eva, I saw motion to my left. Mark's dad had entered through the back door and was standing in the door of the office that led to the kitchen. He startled me. I thought it was Mark.

"Gosh, you scared me!" I snapped at him. "Why would you do that? That's not funny."

Then I noticed the look on his pale face.

"What?" I said. "What?"

He shook his head slowly. "Mark's in the garage, and he's dead."

Eva bolted out the front door, shrieking.

I ran out after her and hurdled the split-rail fence where Cory was waiting with the four-wheeler running. I grabbed the key from the machine and screamed.

Cory jumped off the machine. "No!" he cried. "No, this can't be!"

I threw up. *How could this be?* I thought. *This can't be happening. I have to see for myself.*

I ran as fast as I could down the road toward the cottage. I didn't even think about my kids following me, but that was exactly what they did. I had to see for myself. I had to see my husband. I was hoping I would wake up from this nightmare.

I got to the cottage driveway and found police cars everywhere, yellow crime scene tape cordoning off the garage area, and the garage door open. My car, the dark red Conquest, had been backed in. A silver dryer pipe was coming out the tail pipe and running into the back window, which had been sealed with cardboard. Mark, wearing the blue and black Columbia ski jacket that I had given him a few years earlier for Christmas, was in the driver's seat, just sitting there like he was asleep.

I ran toward the car, but a policewoman grabbed me before I could get to Mark. I squirmed to break free from her grip, cursing her out and begging her to let me go down there. I wanted to see him, touch him, and hold him. I began to sob, and a police officer who knew Mark and me walked up the driveway, opened his arms up, and let me collapse in them. My heart was breaking.

I had totally forgotten that my children had followed me. They were at the top of the driveway with their grandfather, sobbing hysterically. I slowly walked back up to them and held them.

"He quit the team," Cory said in disbelief. "How could he, Mom? He quit the team."

Mark's dad then walked over to me. "You know you're not going to get any life insurance now, don't you?"

Still in shock, I couldn't process what he had said. I took my children over to the neighbors' house so we could sit down and pull ourselves together. I realized I had to make some fast decisions. I would need to arrange a funeral, write an obituary, and so on. A police liaison, a Native American woman of Menominee descent, came over and offered to get the ball rolling. She was middle-aged with long dark hair and was slim and pretty. She took me in her arms, hugged me, and would eventually guide us into a waiting vehicle that would take us back to the lake house. I liked her immediately. I *needed* her. She knew exactly how to help us without being too intrusive.

I gave her our pastor's name and the name of the priest at Cory's parochial school, and everything just started falling into place. I was so angry at Mark's dad that I couldn't think straight. Just minutes after making his unbelievably insensitive comment about the insurance, he started pressuring me to make decisions. He had gone into crisis-management mode, ignoring his own shock and disregarding my feelings. Little did he know that in the days and weeks to come he would be unable to control the situation, make it better, or ignore his own role in Mark's death.

While I was making arrangements with the liaison officer, my daughter ran home, grabbed her cell phone, and called my sister Lizzy at the farm. Lizzy had been waiting with her bags packed and her breath held, praying we would find Mark alive. When she heard Eva's sobs, she jumped into her car and headed for the lake, knowing she would need to be our support system. On her way out of town she pulled into a gas station in shock. She was pumping gas when her father-in-law saw her, put his arms around her, and let her cry. She was then able to get on the road and head north. I was fortunate to have someone like Lizzy in my life, someone who could put her own grief or agenda on hold and just be there, strong and supportive. My second oldest sibling, Lizzy has always been ready and willing to help carry the burdens of others.

Eva then returned and informed me that Lizzy was on her way. Next we called Charlie in San Francisco, where he was living now, and told him what had happened. Between sobs we told him to book a flight ASAP. He was so upset that he tore his apartment apart while he was trying to pack a bag. Shocked and overwhelmed with grief, he finally had to call on his friends for help, and they dutifully booked his flight, took care of all the details, and drove him to the airport.

While we waited for the coroner to come and remove Mark's body from the car, I began reviewing what had happened. I needed some answers. I remembered what Eva had said about Aaron—that he knew something. Something had happened.

"Mark is dead," I said as soon as he answered his phone. "What the hell happened? I know you lied to me."

He began to cry.

"What happened?" I asked again, ignoring his reaction to the news that Mark was dead. I didn't care about him at this point. I just needed some answers.

Haltingly Aaron recounted the story of my husband's last days.

Mark had met up with his buddies at the snowmobile show on Thursday night, and afterward the group had hit the bars. At closing time Mark had been in no shape to drive, but he had remembered my pleas to go home early and let the dog out and had insisted on leaving. At some point during the forty-five-minute drive home, he had pulled off Highway 29 and onto a country road in order to relieve his full bladder. But in the process he had managed to park on a soft shoulder and had ended up stuck in the snow.

First he tried to call Cory, but his phone was either off or the batteries were dead. Next he tried Aaron. His buddy answered his phone and drove off in search of him, but he couldn't find him. Meanwhile, Mark tried knocking on the door of the nearest house. The occupants didn't answer, but they did call the police. Minutes later Mark failed a breathalyzer and was hauled off in handcuffs while his car was towed to Burlington. After he spent the night in jail, he woke up feeling hungover and humiliated. Aaron picked him up at the jail and found him despondent.

"I'm not going to be able to live with this," he told his buddy. "I'm going to lose my job and my company car, and I know Kandace will leave me. She will not understand this time. I let her down again. I can't start over again."

His friend tried to make light of the situation, hoping he could settle Mark down. "Oh, come on, Mark. You'll wake up tomorrow with two arms and two legs, get through this, and life will go on."

"You don't understand," Mark said.

It was Friday morning, and Mark picked up his car, even though he wasn't supposed to drive it for another twenty-four hours. Then he went home to the lake house. He tried to settle into what needed to be done—taking care of the dog and cat, picking up the boat from storage, working—but struggled to maintain his focus. Something else, something dark was taking control of his mind. When he brought the boat back to the lake house and backed it into the garage, he backed in too fast and rammed the motor into the wall, putting a big hole in the plaster. Then he went back inside and tried to focus on his job. That was when he decided to start making some phone calls. He called me. He called each of his children. He called to say good-bye.

Aaron filled me in on as much as I could listen to before I finally hung up in anger. I couldn't talk to him anymore. I was furious. Why hadn't anyone called me? Why hadn't anyone trusted I could help? Why, why, why? Now it was too late. Mark was gone.

I don't remember how much time passed until the coroner came, but I do remember them removing Mark's body from the car. They wrapped a black tarp around him, gently pulled him from the driver's seat, and placed him on a stretcher. He was then placed in the back of a black hearse and driven away.

The liaison officer took me and the kids back down to the lake house. We were numb. When I walked into the house, the answering machine was lit up with messages. I listened to them briefly; they were all from Mark's company and all work-related.

I was so angry. I immediately dialed Mark's boss's number. "Mark is dead. Call off the company," I said and hung up.

I didn't care about anyone else at this point—just me and the kids. I hadn't even thought about what this was doing to Mark's parents. I just didn't care. I was numb.

Lizzy arrived a couple of hours later. I was so grateful. I began to get phone calls from the funeral home to schedule a family meeting plus instructions on what I would have to do. I also got a call from Pastor Don, the minister at Hope Lutheran Church in the village of Mill Center, a rural area west of Burlington. After he checked to make sure the kids and I were okay, he gave me his cell phone number and said to call if I needed him day or night. A slim six feet tall with light brown hair, Pastor Don was the only minister Mark had ever liked. His sermons were always related to real life, not just religious issues. He never forgot a name, which always impressed Mark. He truly cared about people and was always ready to lend a helping hand, although he was not an enabler. He fought his own battles with depression, making him that much more human and that much more approachable. I had a great deal of respect for him. My kids called him PD.

After I hung up with Pastor Don, I resolved to keep my head together . . . and to keep my family together. I couldn't fall apart.

The next day I realized our taxes were supposed to be picked up and signed. I called our accountant and told her what had happened. She said not to worry; she would file an extension. We could call her when things settled down. She had known Mark for a long time and was saddened by the news.

Eva and Cory had each arranged to get time off from school. We would meet up with Charlie the next day in Burlington and proceed to the funeral home to make the arrangement for the funeral to be on Friday. I was still in a fog, just going through the motions, wondering when I was going to wake up from this nightmare.

When we arrived at Mark's parents' house on Tuesday, I felt bad for ignoring their pain and told them they could join us at the meeting to plan the funeral. So Mark's dad, brother, and sister-in-law joined us along with my sister Lizzy, and my kids. Pastor Don was not pleased. He told Mark's dad to be quiet and let me handle the details. I was so confused. I was just trying to hold everyone together and do the right thing, but I was messing everything up. It was a cluster of a meeting. Pastor Don and the funeral director were frustrated. My kids were angry when we left. I just wanted to run away.

The kids and I went back to the lake house and decided to work on the picture boards and the slideshow for the funeral. I knew the song I wanted to go with the slideshow—"You Were Loved" by Wynona Judd—and Eva went to work finding the CD. It helped to have a purpose and keep busy. I was so grateful for my children at that moment. We looked through all the photo albums, but we couldn't find the most current one. Once we found the CD, which was the *Touched by an Angel* compilation, we played it loudly, opened the front door, and danced on the front porch. The album was a favorite of Mark's, a surprising fact, given his tastes. But at the moment we didn't care. We found comfort in the music and each other.

The next day my other two sisters, Grace and Leah, arrived in town. They were staying at the Comfy Inn in the neighboring town of Birchwood. I didn't really want company, but I know they just wanted to be near us and support us. Leah, my second oldest sister, always looked well put together. She wore her russet-colored hair in a bob, never a hair out of place, and always dressed nicely and wore the perfect amount of makeup. Grace—or Gracie as we called her—was my sister closest to my age. She was a pretty lady with dark hair and big dark brown eyes, and she stood a petite five feet three inches tall. She always looked ten years younger than she really was. Of all my sisters, she was the most genuine and accepting of others. She never judged others, but she held herself to an unachievable standard.

Gracie and Leah offered to come with us to Burlington that day. After they greeted us at the lake house, they looked at the picture boards the kids and I had put together and were mildly upset that there weren't more pictures of my side of the family. I explained that we had been unable to find one of the photo albums and that the missing album had contained most of the photos of my side of the family. I couldn't believe they were making a big deal about something that felt so trivial. I was beginning to resent their presence. My sister Lizzy decided to stay put and work around the house, knowing I would need her when we returned. I took care of some more business in Burlington, visited Mark's family, and made some more phone calls to friends and coworkers to let them know what was going on.

While I was at Mark's parents' house talking to Tom, my brother-in-law, he got a phone call. It was Aaron. I was so angry with him that I had been avoiding him for the past few days. He asked Tom to please ask me if he could come over and talk to me. I relented.

Aaron had grown up in the same neighborhood with my husband, who was five years older, but they hadn't become good friends until adulthood. Mark worked in the financial sector and was an avid snowmobiler and skier. Six feet tall with a medium build and light gray hair, he was always nicely dressed. The two of them had a lot in common. Once Aaron had become Mark's financial guy, they became fast friends. I was also friends with Aaron's wife, Becca. She and I worked together at the Burlington Rec Center. Our families vacationed together occasionally, either hitting the beach or the slopes. Aaron was truly one of the nicest guys I'd ever met.

When he arrived, I walked out to his car, and he immediately broke down in tears. All I could do was hold him. *How can all this be happening?* I wondered. *How can I make everything okay for everyone?*

Once Aaron settled down, we decided to take a walk around the block and talk. He needed to know I was okay. He also desperately needed to figure out what had happened and how Mark could have done something like this. I tried my best to keep my composure, to not be angry, and to make everything okay for him—a pattern of behavior that would eventually take its toll on me.

I had done so much crying that day that I was exhausted. So after Aaron left, we decided to go back to the lake house. On the way back my sisters kept asking me what we were doing for dinner. I was getting frustrated as a result. Why did I have to worry about these things? They were acting like they were on vacation and I was their host. We stopped at the store on the way home and shopped. I had been crying so much that I hadn't eaten or drunk anything all day, and now I was pushing a shopping cart around the store while in a daze, trying to make a plan for dinner. When I turned the corner by the fresh produce, everything started spinning, and I went down. The next thing I knew, store employees were standing over me, and my sister was holding my hand. I began to cry. I needed to go home so badly. I needed sleep. I needed to disappear.

Meanwhile, my kids were furious at my sisters for dragging me to the store. They needed their mom, and my family was demanding all my attention. How could I make everyone happy?

CHAPTER 7

On Thursday night we had a private showing—a visitation for my immediate family and Mark's immediate family. My family was upset because I insisted only my siblings and their spouses could attend and that their children should stay home. I didn't want it to become a circus, and it would have become one because I had such a huge family. I wanted there to be a sense of dignity when we said good-bye to Mark for the last time.

After we arrived at the funeral home in Burlington, we took a seat in the hall, where several blue chairs were lined up along the wall.

Eva gave me a strange look. "I've been here before," she said. "I've sat on these blue chairs. I've had this vision, Mom."

It gave me the chills. She, too, had been given a glimpse of Mark's death before it had actually happened. She didn't want to go in and view Mark, but I forced her to. I wanted my kids to have some closure, and I thought in order to do that they needed to say good-bye to their father. To this day I don't know if it was the right thing to do, but I was numb and in shock. My whole world had been turned upside down. I almost felt as though I was living outside my body, like none of what was happening was real. I was stuck in a nightmare and couldn't wake up.

During the viewing I stared at Mark but didn't recognize him. It was this cold, hard body, not the man I had known. Physically there might have been a resemblance to him, but that indefinable thing that made him who he was—his spirit—was gone, and I felt like I was looking at an empty shell. It was not my husband. At this point I couldn't even cry. I held all three of my children and let them cry.

Most of my family was staying at the hotel, and they were all waiting for us in a hospitality room after the viewing. Everything seemed surreal. I almost felt like they were having a party. They had pizza and snacks and beverages of all kinds. I was like a walking zombie. I was there, and yet I wasn't. Greeting people and making inane small talk was like walking a tight rope. It was impossible.

<hr />

As if taking a cue from my leaden heart, Friday morning dawned misty, cloudy, and gray. Seconds after I arrived at the church, I had to use the ladies' room because I was suddenly sick to my stomach. I felt broken in body and spirit.

When I came back out, I stood in front of the casket. And then it hit me.

Oh my God, I thought. *This was the vision.*

I had stood in that exact spot, looking at that exact casket. From that moment on everything transpired as it had in my vision. It was like watching a movie I had already seen. I had been there. I knew there was a reason I'd had the vision, that it wasn't some random occurrence. In retrospect, I'm certain the vision had been a warning to me to trust my gut. *Do something*, it had tried to tell me, *or this will be the result.* But I had paid no attention to the signs and had just let our lives continue on as they always had. I had ignored my inner voice and let everything unfold the way it had unfolded. Even though nothing had felt right during the last four years, I had done nothing to change my life, which had felt like a runaway train headed for disaster.

During the service Pastor Don asked us to stand, and we did. I was seated in the front row with my kids. My legs started shaking so badly I had to sit down. My entire body was overcome with this strange shaking feeling, this energy pulsating through me. Afterward we walked out behind the casket.

A reception at the church followed with food and people—so many people. They kept coming one after the other, and I had no choice but to talk to them all. They became a blur.

At one point Mark's recreational hockey team, the Old Timers, took me, the kids, and Mark's family into a separate room, and we stood in a circle as they dedicated some stupid hockey stick to us like it was some special honor or award in memory of my husband. Mark along with his father and two brothers had played for years on the team, which belonged to an old-time league and was composed of players who were forty years old and older. Mark had known many of his teammates since his youth and had been quite tight with them.

As far as I was concerned, hockey was part of the perfect storm that had claimed my husband's life. I had never liked how much Mark drank and partied with the team. The shallow ceremony pulled me and my family away from the luncheon and the four hundred or so people who wanted to pay their respects to us. I was incensed. Did they really think they were so important in Mark's life that he would have wanted them to run roughshod over his memorial service?

When we returned to the reception room, I saw my father-in-law standing on a platform and pounding the hockey stick on the podium to get everyone's attention, like it was a wedding or something. He thanked everyone for coming and then told a joke. The man had been inappropriate many times, but this time . . . it was just too much. I was devastated. I couldn't believe he was standing up there, trying to be funny. He was once again trying to take control.

Pastor Don, noticing how distraught I was, put his arms around me and guided me from the room. He was angry that this man had done something so rude and inconsiderate. Right then I realized this was what my life had always been like while I had been living with this family. They had always been like an albatross around my neck. They always had to be in control of everyone and everything. Even at my husband's funeral, the kids and I weren't allowed to let things be as we wanted them; Mark's dad had to have the last word. How was I going to survive being in this family without Mark? I was filled with loathing and hatred.

The following week became about wrapping up funeral details—sending out thank-you notes, picking up ashes, paying bills. I was still numb, a walking zombie, still trying to process what my life was going to be like without Mark. So much of me had become about taking care of Mark. I almost didn't know who I was without him. I knew I was going to get lost. I knew it was going to get worse.

Before Charlie went back to San Francisco, we had to get together at my brother-in-law's house to write thank-you notes with Mark's parents. With our respective lists of people to thank, we sat down together and wrote out the notes and addressed them. When my mother-in-law and sister-in-law started bickering at the table, a can of spray starch that was sitting on my sister-in-law's counter fell on the floor for no apparent reason. No one was nearby. No one had jolted the counter. Everybody stopped fighting and stared at it.

Okay, Mark, I thought, *we'll stop fighting.* We kind of laughed it off, but then I thought about my kids, who had gone to run a few errands and were driving around with Mark's ashes in the backseat of the car. I knew he was there with us and didn't want to see us fight.

That was the first piece of physical evidence I had that Mark was still with us.

The next day Charlie and I sat on the dock and talked about what life was going to be like now. It was strange. But at the same time it was nice to reconnect with my oldest son, who was due to fly home the following day. I didn't know how I was going to put him on a plane and send him all the way to the West Coast. It was so far away. He would have to grieve without his family. Eva and Cory had to go back to their everyday lives too. Though she'd had no time to study, Eva would have to face finals week.

When Charlie boarded his plane the next day, he was coming down with the flu. It was all I could do to say good-bye; I just wanted to take care of him.

After he left, I came down with the same flu bug. I felt like I was going to die. As I rested on the couch, I wondered how I was going to recuperate, much less function. Then I felt someone rubbing my head. I wasn't asleep. My eyes were wide open. As I lay there, I felt this gentle rubbing over and over again. It actually felt like the hair on top of my head was moving. It was comforting. I became lost in the sensation. Afterward I wondered what I had just experienced. What was it? What was going on?

Meanwhile, Mark's company wanted us to box up all his work-related papers and files. It was a huge job, one the company wanted us to complete in two weeks, at which time they would come for the files and Mark's company car. We would need all that time to sort through everything in his desk. I also had to look through his financial files, retrieve his passwords for online use, and fill out insurance paperwork.

At the end of the week Eva came home to check on me. Along with being worried about me, she was still numb and couldn't function around people at school. She tried to sit in her dad's chair, his oversized La-Z-Boy recliner, but again she felt a strange energy, a vibration that made her jump to her feet.

A few days later Mark's middle brother barged into my kitchen and went straight to the great room. "I have to sit in this chair,"

Harry said and proceeded to get comfortable in Mark's recliner. "I have to sit in this chair."

I kept looking at him and thinking that I just wanted everyone out of my house. I didn't want people around me. I simply couldn't deal with it.

And what was with the chair? It seemed we all had a strange connection to it. My favorite memories of it involved both Mark and me, the way I would crawl onto his lap, my legs folded on each side of his thighs, and give him a giant hug. We had fit perfectly in that chair together.

CHAPTER 8

My kids and I were working in Mark's office one night when I decided to go to bed because I was exhausted. It was ten o'clock, and I didn't have the energy to sort through one more pile or look through one more file. I knew we were running out of time to pack up his office for his company, but the magnitude of the project was overwhelming. Only the foyer separated my bedroom from Mark's office on the first floor, and as I tried to fall asleep, I could hear Cory and Eva rummaging through papers, opening and closing drawers, searching for clues. The project for them was more about finding closure—and perhaps gaining some insight into their father's mind-set before he had taken his own life—than it was about simply boxing up his office.

"Why did Dad save all this stuff?" Eva asked. "Look, here are some Father's Day cards we gave him. Oh, my God. Here's a letter I wrote to Santa."

They shared a belly laugh.

Then the room fell silent, and seconds later they were bursting into my room with a yellow piece of paper from a legal pad. They had found it among the religious psalms, prayers, and assorted cards and letters in one of the drawers.

"Look, Mom!" Eva said excitedly after she flipped on the light. "Dad wrote a suicide note on May 20, 2004."

I sat up in bed, took the note in my hand, and noticed after reading a few lines that it read exactly like his final note to us. Only this one wasn't finished. Why had he changed his mind? And why had he been so close then on the eve of Charlie's high school graduation? That year, 2004, had been a rough one for all of us. It was the year we had sold the big old house, the year when Mark had been in such a bad place. That was the year when I'd had the vision of Mark's funeral. It was all starting to make sense to me. I had been shown a picture, a warning of events to come. I had ignored those warnings, and the things I had envisioned had come true. I had never believed in visions or premonitions. I had never thought they were real.

"We were lucky we had him for four more years," I told my kids.

Eva wasn't buying it. "I can't believe he wanted to leave us four years ago!" she said crossly. "How could he be so selfish? Why would he think we didn't need him anymore?"

I tried to soothe her anger, but she stormed upstairs to her room.

Cory returned to his father's office. But rather than risk finding another reminder of his father's inner battle, he logged on to the Internet to chat with friends and listen to music.

I tried to go back to sleep, but less than an hour later strange lights suddenly appeared in the corner of my room. They looked like stars twinkling in the night sky. I opened and shut my eyes several times, trying to adjust my vision, certain my eyes were playing tricks on me. I'd had migraine headaches once or twice before, debilitating headaches that left my vision blurred and stomach upset. But this was different. In fact, since Mark's death I'd had a constant low-grade headache. Even if I took tons of painkillers, it never went away. Sometimes it was worse than at other times, which I chalked up to crying so much.

Now I was seeing lights. I was still fixated on the flickering lights in the corner of my room, watching as they disappeared and reappeared when I noticed the space right beside my bed was moving. The air was wavy and roughly the size of a person. I jumped out of bed and hurried into the foyer, where I was able to see Cory through the office's French doors. He was still seated at Mark's desk, headset on, computer open, and listening to music.

He took off his headset after he noticed me. "You okay, Mom? What's up?"

"I just need to stand here for a few minutes," I said. I was too freaked out to go back into my room. But I kept what I had just seen to myself.

That night marked the beginning of many eerie, restless nights. At first I didn't say anything, but then Eva started talking to me about things that were happening to her at school. Like me, she was having headaches. But she was also having strange dreams. Technically she was only having one dream, which was always the same: Mark wanted to talk to me, and she would tell him I couldn't hear him. Often I was even in her dreams, but I could never hear Mark or see him.

Then *I* began dreaming that Mark was still with us. He was doing the same things he had done when he was alive—snowmobiling or recreating or just being there in the cottage or in the lake house. "You can't be here," I kept telling him in my dreams. "You're dead." But he would never talk to me. He was just there, living life with us. The frightening part was that it didn't feel like a dream at all; it felt all too real. Then I would wake up and once again have to face the reality of Mark's death.

When my daughter and I started comparing notes, we realized we always had the same dream on the same night. Mark was always in the same clothes, the blue and black Columbia ski jacket, Levi's jeans, and hiking boots he had died in, and the dreams were always at the same location, usually either the cottage or the lake house. I finally told her about the flashing lights.

"Oh, my God," she said. "I see the same lights too."

I couldn't believe it. We were experiencing the same things, *dreaming* the same things. Then we began noticing other phenomena.

Things moved around. Pictures fell. I found lost items. Doors that had been unlocked were suddenly locked. I would find the house keys in weird places because I kept forgetting to lock the doors at night, which would have driven Mark crazy.

It took weeks to get Mark's personal belongings back, and when I did, the smell of the car exhaust was all over his clothes. It was so overpowering it actually burned my eyes. I ended up having to throw everything out. Conspicuously absent from his returned personal belongings was the garage door opener he had taken from the Impala the afternoon we had switched cars. There should have been two openers in the Conquest, but I had found just one the very next day after we'd found Mark's body. Had the police misplaced the extra one? If not, it was possible it had been stolen. If that were the case, I would have to get the garage door opener code changed as soon as possible. The kids and I combed through the Impala repeatedly in an attempt to ease my mind. When that failed, we searched the house. But we never found the missing garage door opener. Then one day after I returned from the grocery store, I pulled into the driveway, looked to my right, and there it was, sitting on the passenger's seat next to me. What was going on?

Three weeks after Mark's death we tried to settle back into some semblance of a normal life. I went back to work as the volunteer manager at the Greater Burlington Rec Center. My goal was to wrap things up before summer, when things would slow down. I tried to engage my brain with work. I tried to be with people. But it was impossible. I kept falling apart and having meltdowns. I couldn't function. I needed professional help. In early June I asked my boss for a leave of absence, and she readily granted it with the stipulation that I return in mid-August.

I spent the next two months at the lake, trying to figure out what we were going to do. Were we going to stay, or were we going to sell the house? I also wanted to know if Cory would be okay living in the house with me but without his dad. He was angry all the time and yelled at me constantly. I didn't know how I was going to survive.

My relationship with Mark's family became even more trying. They were leaning on me and using me as an outlet for their grief. For some reason they felt it necessary to talk about everyone else who had died by suicide, or they would tell me about a comment someone had made. I couldn't stand to see them. I couldn't stand to even be in the same room with them. Every time I saw them, reality hit me in the face—they were ill, and so was I.

At my wit's end I asked Cory if he would be more comfortable living in Burlington for the school year. Each of us would enjoy a much easier commute. I also had a hunch that we could each benefit from a change of scenery. As beautiful as it was, the lake simply reminded us on a daily basis of everything we'd been through. Cory agreed to the move, so I found us an apartment. The building was generic, colorless like our world. But it was clean and light, and it felt easy. Although I wouldn't need it until mid-August, just before school started, I began renting it on June 15 in order to hold it. We would still be living at the lake house for the time being, but we'd be able to start furnishing the apartment now, which would make the coming transition easier.

Eva had decided to stay in Burlington for the summer so she could either find a job or take a class. She ended up driving back and forth between the lake house and Burlington, paying rent and feeling sad all the time. She vacillated between thinking she would be better off at home and then thinking she would be better off at school. It was crazy. We were all trying to find our way. Some of my family came up to spend a little time with me to see how I was doing. Their visits were nice, but it was always hard for me to try to entertain guests or try to act like I was okay. I felt like I wasn't alive anymore, like I was an inanimate object just standing there among the living. I wanted to be with Mark. I wanted to die. I didn't know how to live and take care of everyone and be the person everyone needed and wanted me to be. I needed someone to take care of me, but there was no one. I had ignored what living with Mark's illness had done to me, but now that he was gone, I couldn't ignore it anymore.

CHAPTER 9

I was still having constant headaches, still losing weight, and still having the dreams. Mark was still there too, living with us as though he were still alive. My mood was always bad; I was in a constant state of anger and frustration. I woke up agitated every morning because I didn't understand how my husband could still be there in my dreams at night and not be there when I woke up. The dreams were a constant reminder of what I had lost.

Mark's family became even more needy and in my face. Eva and I were fighting as we went through all of Mark's toys and belongings, trying to decide which things we should sell. Meanwhile, Cory seemed determined to live his father's life. It was almost as though he was trying to take his place. When he couldn't fix something or something wasn't going his way, he would have a huge meltdown, and with each meltdown he took me with him. I was also worried about all the money Eva was spending while running back and forth to Burlington. She didn't have a job, and she wouldn't see a counselor.

Everything fell apart on Fourth of July weekend, at which time Eva and I had a huge fight. She told me I needed help and that I couldn't talk to her about the things that were going on because she couldn't handle it. The only person I could talk to, the only person I could bounce things off of had just turned me down. After our argument I walked back up to the lake house from the beach, went into my room, and smashed my wedding photo. I then took a shard of glass with me into the shower and held it to my wrist. I sat there on the shower bench with the glass against my wrist, trying so hard to find the courage to do exactly what Mark had done. I was sobbing hysterically. I wanted to leave it all behind.

Then something snapped. I couldn't do it. I got out of the shower, went back into the bedroom, and literally destroyed my closet. Then I took all of Mark's clothes, threw them into a big pile, put some of my clothes in a bag, and took off without talking to Eva or Cory.

It was late afternoon as I drove into Burlington, and not much was open because of the holiday. I stopped at Tony's, a little Italian sub shop in the village of Hope, and picked up a large Italian beef and cheese sub. Then after I bought a bottle of white Riesling from a nearby liquor store, I drove to the apartment, which was still empty—no furniture, no food, no dishes, just a bed with a few sheets and blankets. I parked in the one-stall garage and then unlocked the apartment and went inside. To my right was a small dinette area and kitchen. On the other side of a raised snack bar was the living room, and down the hall were two bedrooms, one with an attached bathroom and another bathroom with laundry facilities. I stepped from the living room out onto the balcony, which overlooked a wild, grassy marsh, and sat down to think.

After I opened a blank journal my girlfriend at work had given me, I poured my heart out onto the page. Desperate and suicidal, I needed to make sense of how I felt and where I was going. My kids kept calling me and texting me, but I ignored them.

Suspecting I might be in town, they eventually drove to the apartment and found me. I told them I was fine but that I planned to spend the rest of the weekend alone at the apartment. I couldn't come back to the lake—not yet. They were understandably upset. Eva was twenty years old now. Cory was only seventeen. They were still quite raw and vulnerable and couldn't understand why I couldn't be there for them. Would I ever be their mother again? The question seemed open to debate. I knew that I was failing them, that I was failing my duties as a mother. But I knew that if I didn't get out of the lake house and away from the family, I would die. I was doing what I had to do to survive, to save my own life.

Mark's father was pouring gasoline on the fire as usual. After Eva and Cory found me at the apartment, they told me what he had said to them before they had left to search for me:

"Be prepared to find her dead."

We were all hurting. We were all doing and saying stupid things. But to this day I find what he said to them beyond the pale. It was symptomatic of the dysfunctional dynamics routinely at play in Mark's family. I couldn't take them or their unhealthiness any longer. In fact, I felt like I didn't know how to do life without Mark. I certainly didn't know how to cope with his family.

After my children drove back to the lake house, I returned to my journal. I needed the outlet. I needed to be alone. I needed to escape, if only for one weekend. As I filled page after page with thoughts and feelings, I recognized the fact that I needed help. I also acknowledged what had become obvious: Mark was still with me. But how? I had never really believed in spirits or communication between the dead and the living. Neither had Mark.

"When you're dead," he used to say, "you're dead. There isn't anything after this."

"Are you sure?" I would ask. "There has to be something after."

We had never really agreed on what we believed. I wasn't even sure if Mark had believed in God or the divine. I had been with him for almost thirty years but had never fully understood his religious beliefs, which remained a mystery after his death. We had raised our children Lutheran, but he had usually only attended church when I forced the issue. In his last few years he had begun attending

Catholic Mass on occasion, which was a return to his childhood faith. Perhaps he had been searching.

In any case my beliefs would shortly be tested. What I thought I knew about death, about where you go after you pass on—all my assumptions would be challenged. By spending the Fourth of July weekend alone at the apartment with only my journal to keep me company, I was opening myself up to a new journey, a new purpose. The road ahead was a rough one, but ultimately it would lead to a healing place.

I'm not sure how I even got through the rest of that summer. At one point in July I was so ill that I walked into a nurse practitioner's office in Batton, a small town about fifteen minutes from the lake house. After I sat down, I immediately said, "I need help."

"Do you feel like hurting yourself?" the nurse practitioner asked.

"Yes," I answered.

She knew all about Mark's suicide and what our family was going through. She had seen Eva when she'd had mono and a variety of female ailments. This was my first attempt to reach out for help. She put me on Lexapro, an antidepressant, and some antianxiety drugs, but all the Lexapro did was make me feel lethargic and more depressed, though it did stop me from wanting to hurt myself. The antianxiety medication helped me sleep, which was a good thing since I wasn't sleeping much. When I did sleep, I had such horrible dreams that I would wake up with painful knots in my neck. I still had terrible headaches that showed no signs of going away, and I was continuing to lose weight.

I didn't stay on Lexapro long, but I kept taking the antianxiety medication so I could get more rest. Eva, too, was on antianxiety medication. We made it through the summer as best we could by simply taking one day at a time—a survival tactic.

In August the kids decided to get tattoos in memory of their dad. I'm not a big fan of tattoos, and at the time I wanted them to take some more time and think over their decision. But I totally understood the impulse. After they agreed to go through with it, they put their heads together and designed a cross with the words *Forever Loved, Never Forgotten* emblazoned on it. Eva had hers tattooed on the top of her foot, and Cory had his inscribed on his chest. They actually turned out nice. I liked them. Charlie decided to do something way bigger. He tattooed Mark's senior high school photo on his arm. The photo looked eerily like Charlie.

If you can't beat them, I thought, *join them*. I designed a tattoo to go on the inside of my ankle . . . for my eyes only. Like Eva and Cory's, it was a cross with the words *Forever Loved, Never Forgotten* inscribed on it. I had it done at an ink shop in downtown Burlington by a tattoo artist by the name of Tyler, who had also done the kids' designs. It hurt like hell but not as bad as it hurt to lose Mark.

CHAPTER 10

That summer I began seeing a counselor, a middle-aged, soft-spoken man named Jay who stood a slim six feet tall. At our first session he asked a lot of questions and talked far too much about hockey. This made me distrust him at first, but Cory, who was also seeing him, hit it off with him immediately *because* he was a hockey dad. He reminded Cory of his father. After my first visit with Jay I left my journal with him so he could read it. He called me that night to check on me, saying that after he had read my journal, he understood the dark place I was in and was concerned about me. This won me over. Knowing that he genuinely wanted to help me allowed me to trust him.

But I was a long way from healing. On August 20, a Wednesday night, I wanted to die again. I was trying to be a good mom—trying to cook, trying to look after my children, and trying to hold our family together. I had even returned to work a few days earlier. But none of my efforts bore fruit. With everything crashing down around me, I took off driving. By now Cory and I had moved into the apartment, and Eva was getting ready to go back for another year of college.

Not surprisingly I ended up back at the lake house. Although the apartment was our home now, we still planned to visit the lake house on weekends and holidays. I sat on the screened porch, sipped a beer, and pictured myself floating on the lake before sinking, sinking, sinking to the peaceful bottom. I would join Mark, and the pain would finally be gone. I knew Cory and Eva would be worried about me. They along with my siblings knew how precariously close I'd already come to taking my own life. So why was I putting them through this? Why was I being such a lousy mom? The more I ruminated over the downward spiral I was caught in, the more I thought I didn't want to be a mom anymore. I no longer had the skills. Although others would try to help me, I knew there was nothing anyone could do. No one could help me but me. I had to find a way to pull myself up.

Cory finally got a hold of me, and I apologized for taking off and leaving him alone to worry about me again.

"I'm trying," I said. "It's the best I can do right now. It's all I can do to just hold it all together."

Cameron, Lizzy's daughter, who was just seven years younger than me, came out for the weekend and stayed with us at the lake house. It was a beautiful place to host family and friends, but I could hardly bring myself to entertain a visitor. I was too consumed by my own despair.

On Saturday night the four of us—Cameron, Eva, Cory, and me—sat on the screened porch and chatted. It felt good to share a few good laughs, and the kids seemed better, more like themselves. As the evening wore on, Cameron and the kids named my dark side Norma. The kids didn't like Norma, who was sad, mad, crazy, and sometimes mean. Eva didn't realize it, but she had the power to invoke Norma. Anytime she was demanding, selfish, or insensitive, Norma reared her ugly head. When Norma made an appearance, I couldn't be anyone's mom. Norma wanted only to die. I tried to suppress her, but when I felt overwhelmed or like I was losing control, she always surfaced. I later told Jay, my counselor, about her, and he seemed amused that my kids and niece would name my dark side. But naming it gave me a clearer understanding of that part of me . . . and something to work on.

The end of August marked the beginning of Eva's sophomore year at UVM. Cory and I loaded up the Suburban and helped her move in. Then the three of us drove back to the lake house so she could take her own car back when school started. During the drive home a mallard duck flew straight at us and shattered the Suburban's windshield. We got off the highway and pulled into a gas station, where the three of us burst into tears. Tiny shards of glass covered Eva's legs and knees, and as we carefully plucked them from her clothing, we realized how lucky she was to have been reclining at the moment of impact. Had she been sitting upright, she would have been hit in the face with glass. Compared to what we had been through, it was a minor incident for everyone but the duck. But the accident served as a reminder of how fragile we all were.

Meanwhile, Cory was about to begin his junior year of high school. While I immersed myself in the busy season at my job, he whipped himself into shape for preseason hockey. Cory missed Mark terribly—the two had spent endless hours on the ice together—but rather than empathize with the pain he felt, his hockey coach simply admonished him not to quit, lest he disappoint his late father. It was a struggle for me to be involved in the hockey community in any way, but thankfully several of our friends stepped up and supported Cory however they could.

By now we were spending almost all of our time at the apartment. The lake house had begun to feel empty and deserted. But the short commute and close proximity to Cory's school and friends greatly reduced our stress load. Less time on the road meant more time with friends and family. Unfortunately when I wasn't at work, I was often at the apartment, alone and depressed.

When September rolled around, I drove to the lake to pick up some fall decorations and some fall clothes. With Cory away at a hockey tournament with his friends, I decided to stay overnight. But the minute I walked inside, all the bad memories came flooding back. There was something about the lake house, something wrong, something . . . *evil*.

I spent a few minutes going through Mark's things in his office. Then I put on his sunglasses and watch and retreated to the living room, where I lay down on the floor to think about him. When I sat up, my head started pounding, and the whole room began to fill with the smell of carbon monoxide. My eyes burned. I stood up and walked up the flight of stairs overlooking the great room.

"You can't be here," I said aloud. "I can't come here and spend time in this house if you're going to be here, knocking over stuff and going where you don't belong." I was frightened. "What do you want? Why are you still here?"

I went down into the basement and was hit by another wave of carbon monoxide. That was enough to convince me I couldn't stay there anymore. "I'm not staying," I told Mark. I packed up the stuff I had come to get, locked up the house, got into the car, and drove back to Burlington.

When I got back to the apartment, I called Aaron and told him what had happened.

"Well," he said, "we're having friends over tomorrow to watch the football game. You should come over."

Sunday morning I decided that I might take him up on his invitation. I went to the mall to try to find some new clothes. I had lost so much weight—between fifteen and twenty pounds since Mark had died—that nothing fit any longer. I was at the mall in The Gap dressing room when my phone rang. It was my security system company, which informed me that the alarm was going off at the lake house.

I was shocked. "Has anyone broken in?"

"No," the tech dispatcher answered, "it's your motion detectors that are triggering your alarm."

"Then call my in-laws," I suggested. "They're out there."

"We did, but they either don't have a key or couldn't find one. They walked around but didn't see anything out of place."

What's going on? I wondered. I would have to go up there and make sure everything was all right and then reset the alarm. I left the mall and drove up to the lake, puzzled by what had happened. I had just been there the day before, and everything had been fine.

When I got there, I went inside, looked around, and saw nothing wrong. Everything was in its place. I even looked around to see if some animal or maybe a mouse had set off the alarm. But when I asked the security people if that was possible, they said it wasn't. I knew they were right because we'd had a cat and a dog, and neither one of them had set off the alarm.

I reset the alarm and then drove to my in-laws to tell them where the key was and to just say hello because I knew I'd feel bad if I didn't. I had never had much of a relationship with them and didn't even talk to them on a regular basis. All I was trying to do was survive, and I wasn't doing a very good job.

As soon as I walked through my in-laws' door, they started to badger me.

"Why don't you call? Why don't we ever see you? We feel like we've lost five people and not just one."

My mother-in-law started crying. "Your father-in-law is going to have a heart attack because of this," she said. "Because of *you*."

They went on and on, telling me what the priest had said, that they would be better in a year. I couldn't take any more. I was barely holding it together . . . and now this. I was being bombarded, accused, made to feel like I was responsible for Mark's death and the health of everyone involved. Norma was about to make another appearance.

"Do you know what?" I said. "I'm just trying to get through one day at a time—that's all. I can't do any more than that. Whatever is going on with me has nothing to do with you."

I then told my father-in-law he should get some counseling.

"What for?" he asked. "What would I say?"

It was another reminder of what I was living with. I knew if I didn't extricate myself from his codependent family, I would probably be destroyed just like Mark had been.

Norma was back. I went home and never did go to Aaron's place to watch the football game and socialize. Norma wanted one of two things—to be alone or to be with Mark for eternity.

When I got up the next morning to go to work, I turned on my phone and learned I had several new messages from the security company and my in-laws. The alarm was still going off, so I had to go back to the lake. Once again I found nothing out of place at the lake house, no sign of anything that might be causing the alarm to go off. However, I wasn't alone this time. I had asked a representative from the security company to meet me there since I couldn't keep trekking out to the lake every time an alarm went off.

"Could energy be setting off the motion sensors?" I asked him. "Like a lot of energy?"

The security rep, a short, heavyset, balding man, had known Mark and went to our church, Hope Lutheran.

"Absolutely," he said. "That's what they pick up on—motion, energy, and heat."

"You're going to think I'm crazy," I said, "but when I was up here on Saturday, I could smell Mark. I could *feel* him. He knocked his picture frame over. I know he was here and that he's still around."

"I totally believe that could be setting off your alarms," he said.

We proceeded to disconnect the motion sensors. If anyone tried to break into the house, we reasoned, they'd still have to get past the sensors on the doors and windows. Fortunately we never had to deal with any more false alarms after that.

Our dreams, Eva's and mine, became more disturbing. In one Mark would be in the car and would turn the ignition on and off continuously. In another he would look horribly ill and appear almost demonic with blood gushing from his zombielike eyes. Eva would tell him that he couldn't stay in the lake house anymore and that he had to leave, and he would respond by telling her that he had to talk to me. Every conversation they had ended with Eva telling him I couldn't hear him. In my dreams I could always see him, but I couldn't hear him.

The dreams no longer seemed like dreams. It was more like we were watching him—wherever he was. We weren't sure what to do. We knew he was still around, that we were not just dreaming about him. I still saw the wavy air on occasion, a truly frightening phenomenon. Growing sicker by the day, I had already lost more than twenty-five pounds. I looked like a walking skeleton, a skeleton that no longer recognized its reflection. I had become a stranger to myself.

CHAPTER 11

*E*very time I passed my desk while at the apartment, a little community newspaper would be on the floor. It would always be open and showing an ad for a psychic in Burlington. I would pick up the newspaper, close it, and put it on my desk, and the next time I walked by, it would be on the floor again, open to that ad.

I didn't give the newspaper or the ad too much thought. Work kept me busy that fall as did my family and my volunteer work. The kids and I volunteered to help out at the rec center for a five-kilometer fun run at the Cornerstone Community Ice Center in Burlington on Thanksgiving morning, and we had to show up at 4:30 a.m., well before dawn. By the time we got home around eleven that morning, we were all exhausted. The kids took a nap while I got food ready for Thanksgiving dinner at Tom and Sue's house.

I was in the apartment's tiny kitchen when I saw a dark figure whoosh down the hall after the kids. *Oh, my God!* I thought. *It's Mark.* I was certain it was him. He was still with us, still living with me as he had done when he was alive, still drawing strength from my energy. I couldn't help thinking that he must be growing weaker along with me.

At Tom and Sue's place that night we sat down to a Thanksgiving dinner with Mark's parents and his younger brother, Harry. We all pretended we were okay, but it was the saddest Thanksgiving any of us had ever spent together. We stayed just long enough to eat and then headed back to the apartment.

Eva returned to school at the end of the Thanksgiving weekend, and not long afterward Cory had an utter meltdown. Playing hockey without his father, going on with life—it was all too much. He went to his room, sobbing.

I sat down on a green chair in the living room, frustrated. But a moment later I felt someone's arm around me. I could literally feel the weight of it on my opposite shoulder. Weary and miserable just a moment earlier, I was smiling now. I wasn't alone. I sat still and let whoever it was that had this arm around me comfort me.

The following day Gracie, my sister closest to my age, called to check in on me, and I told her I thought I'd seen Mark in the apartment and that he was still with me. Then I told her about the arm around me.

"Yeah?" she said. "I had a dream last night. Do you know whose arm was around your shoulder?"

"No," I said.

"It was Dad."

My father had died when I was eight.

"I dreamed it last night," Grace continued, "and I knew. You were sitting in a green chair, and he was sitting beside you with his arm around you."

"Oh, my God," I said in a hushed voice.

"Now that you think you're seeing Mark," she added, "I have to tell you what my coworker said a couple weeks ago."

"Your coworker?"

"One of my coworkers walked into my office on your birthday. She asked me why I looked so sad, and I told her it was because I knew it was your first birthday since Mark's death. That's when she said she had something important to tell me. It turns out that she lost her son a couple of years ago, and a while back some friends told her about an opening at this gallery where some medium was going to be making an appearance. They asked her to go, and she went along just for the heck of it. The first thing the medium said was that there was a gentleman there, a middle-aged gentleman who had taken his own life. He had passed away on April 13th and was desperately trying to connect with someone. Nobody who was there responded to the medium, and the medium went on to say that the man was very agitated and hadn't crossed over yet. He desperately needed to connect with someone there. The medium kept asking if anyone knew what she was talking about, but no one did.

"Anyway, my coworker wanted to know when Mark had died, so I told her, 'Well, technically he died on April 13th, but they didn't find him until the 14th, so his death certificate says the fourteenth, and so did the obituary. Everybody thinks he died on Monday, April 14th, but he died on April 13th, a Sunday.' When I told her that, she said, 'Oh, my God! You need to tell your sister that her husband came through at the gallery and that he's trying to talk to her.' She gave me the medium's name—Lily—and said you should consider seeing her. She's in Crystal Falls."

"Wow," I said, not sure how much stock to put in the conversation.

I took the information from Grace, and at my next session with Jay, my counselor, I relayed the story to him.

He leaned back in his chair with a thoughtful expression on his face. "What are you going to do with this information?"

"I don't know," I said. I still needed time to absorb everything.

Charlie flew home for Christmas, joining Eva, Cory, and me at the lake house. Eva was still having dreams about her father, and one night she had actually seen him sitting at the edge of her bed. Some nights she could feel him rubbing the top of her head.

I had experienced the same thing on nights when I was feeling especially depressed, and when I told her, she insisted we do something to help him.

After Christmas we were at the lake house when I had another nightmare. In it Mark was so ill, so demon like, so tortured with blood coming from his eyes that I joined my daughter in her room.

"I just had a dream," she told me, "and Dad was really sick. He can't stand anymore. I had to make him a bed, a little cot in my closet. He's there now, and he wants to talk to you. You have to help him. You're the only one who can help him. You have to do something about it. You need to go see the medium."

I sobbed. "I'm so ill," I said through tears. "I'm not getting any better."

We talked about Mark and our increasingly troubling dreams, and we agreed that I would never heal as long as he was still there, living off my energy. In fact, it seemed likely I would eventually die if we didn't get help. I decided that night to see Lily, the medium in Crystal Falls. I made an appointment for January 9.

CHAPTER 12

I felt like a crazy person for even considering seeing a medium, but I was desperate. I truly thought I wouldn't survive if I didn't do something. My kids, too, needed me to heal if they were ever going to recover from the blow of their father's suicide. I drove to Barre, where my sister-in-law, Ann, had been working for a few days. She had said she would take the next day off, which was a Friday, and go with me to Crystal Falls.

Ann, my brother Kevin's wife, was a property manager for a state housing program and traveled extensively to manage properties. She lived in Montpelier when she wasn't on the road. She was a large woman who gave hugs like no one's business. As an only child, she had embraced being a part of my huge family, although she sometimes found herself feeling jealous of our closeness since sharing was never easy for her. Like Lizzy, she was a take-charge type of person and was always there when you needed her. She had a contagious belly laugh that made you feel instantly welcome in her home.

We stayed in a hotel right off the expressway near Crystal Falls. Worried about my meeting with the medium the next day, I hardly slept a wink. We awoke to a blinding snowstorm. Petrified and ill, I knew there was no way I could focus on driving in such treacherous conditions.

"I'm going to have to cancel the appointment," I said.

"We're going," Ann replied firmly. "We're not going to let this stop us."

As I would learn in a few hours from Lily, there were evil forces—she would call them cockroaches—that worked against a person's soul, and right now they were trying to keep me away from her. They were bent on destroying me and my family. But I had Ann on my side.

"I truly believe you have to be there," she said. "You have to go. I'll drive."

We got in my car, and she took the wheel. We needed an extra hour and a half to get there; however, by the time we did, the snowstorm had subsided, and the roads were all right.

Lily's small two-story condo was in an ordinary neighborhood on the far west side of Crystal Falls. It looked pretty much exactly like all the other condos in the vicinity and was therefore rather difficult to locate. Inside it was cluttered with angels, candles, crystals, and stones.

Lily, seated with an infant boy on her lap in the living room, embraced me with an unmistakably loving energy that immediately put me at ease. I felt comforted by how overjoyed she was by my visit. It was almost as if she had been waiting eagerly for my arrival. She was an extra-large woman. "Honey, I'm an XXXL," she would later say. But it wasn't her size that grabbed my attention. It was her radiance. A stunning Hawaiian goddess, she had large dark brown eyes that were perfectly framed with dark eyeliner and that were like windows into my own soul, into the universe. Adorned in bling from head to toe, she even had sparkles on her flip-flops.

"Have a seat, baby girl," she said enthusiastically.

I looked at my sister-in-law with tears in my eyes.

"You're going to be all right," Ann said, turning for the door. "I'll wait for you in the car."

I sat down and was greeted by a black cat rubbing against my legs. "It's funny that you called me *baby girl*," I said. "Only people who truly care about me call me that."

"Really?" she said, laughing.

The baby in Lily's lap was her grandson. When we were ready to start, the infant's father appeared and carried the little boy upstairs. Lily then invited me to follow her into a small kitchen and asked me to sit down at a small round table. Crumbs covered the tablecloth.

"Those were awfully good brownies," she quipped.

Next to the crumbs sat an unpretentious box, where the fee was to be deposited . . . without being counted.

Lily asked me for my name and address. She would be recording our session, she explained, and would be sending me a CD of the recording.

When she learned I had come all the way from Burlington, she was amazed. "In all that snow!"

She pushed the record button, and the session began.

"Is there anything you want me to focus on?" she asked. "Because what happens during the session is that I pick up on things you don't even have to tell me about. So if there's something you want me to focus on, this is the time to tell me. Otherwise I'll channel. I'll look at cards, and there will be questions and answers. Since you came all the way from Burlington, I'll give you plenty of time for that. My God, you came all the way from Burlington, woman—in all that snow!"

"I had to," I said. "A woman who was at one of your seminars told me my husband who crossed over recently came to talk to you to try to find someone to connect with."

"Did he come through in the gallery?" Lily asked.

"Yes," I answered.

"That's wonderful," Lily said. "Wow! Did she get a copy of the CD?"

"I don't know."

"Do you remember when the gallery session was?" she asked.

"In November," I said.

"This November? There might be a CD with the information on it, but I don't remember it. That's the thing about me. I don't

81

remember anything I tell people. So I'm really fascinated by this. Well, I'm glad he was able to come through."

"I get the feeling that he hasn't crossed over yet and needs help," I said.

"So he needs a little help," Lily said. "This is how we are going to do this. This is a little different than a gallery. Sometimes I can just see these people. But because you're here specifically about your husband not having fully crossed over, I'm going to try to get in touch with him. What's going to happen is that I'm going to ring this Tibetan bell, and it will raise the vibration in the room and neutralize negativity. And then we'll see if I feel his presence. Usually what I do is I have you say his name at least once, and if it's him, he's going to come in more fully. So let's see what happens. I'm going to go ahead and ring this Tibetan bell, and we'll go from here."

The sound of the piercing bell reverberated in the room. She continued to hit it, and with each hit the sound echoed louder; however, it was followed by a peaceful feeling. It wasn't long before I almost felt as though I was part of the bell. It was in me, and I was inside of it. I could almost feel Mark drawing closer to me with each hit.

"When I'm ringing the bell," Lily explained, "I always say a prayer to the divine and to all the spirit guides and all the others who are assisting me on the other side—angels, guardians, and masters. One of the people that I called in is a very dear friend of mine who crossed within the last year. Her name is Cindy Johnson, and she was known as the psychic astrologer to the stars. She came in right away, and she pointed to your right. And it reminded me of a male figure sitting on a cot, like an army cot. Or at least that's what it made me think of. It wasn't that he was uncomfortable; it just made me think of—Lily struggled for a moment to describe what she was feeling. "I guess it reminded me of someone who wants to be outdoors but at the same time wants to be in a comfortable place. The first thing he did when he came through was get off the cot, which took a lot of effort."

"He's very ill right now," I said. "He needs us to forgive him."

"Okay. Do you recognize that he's in between realms?"

"Yes," I said.

"He's constantly listening to your heart. The reason he hasn't crossed over is because he's listening to your heart and the hearts of the people who love him—that's why. So in this time there have been many expressions of love. Some of them are gestures—touching, comforting, soothing. It's this feeling of—I have to tell you this—as if his soul can't forgive him."

"I know that," I whispered.

"There's something—this is a complicated—'I can't forgive myself,'" Lily said. "It's almost as if he feels the feeling of his soul. I can feel him right here. Whoa—Whoa. He's right here. He's in the gray space. It's called 'the gray space.' This is the thing—" She paused for a second. "I'm going to talk to him directly. This is what I can do. I can go in between realms. I have to get something, and it might be upstairs. I think we can help him. Hold on."

I waited while Lily went in search of the object she needed. All I could think of was Mark and the pain he had to be in—the pain we had all been in these last seven months. I hoped that Lily would be able to help him and the rest of us find peace. I heard her call out for two white stones that were on her altar. Then she returned to the kitchen.

"The gray space is not a comfortable space for me at all," Lily said. "So I have to smudge all around you."

"I know. I know," I said. "I felt where he is."

"I need you to stand up over here and lift your feet one at a time," Lily said.

I lifted one foot, and she told me to lift the other.

"Lift your arms," she said. "Then lift your neck. This is called smudging. If we're going into the gray space, I don't want anything coming out that shouldn't be here. Don't worry. You have angels all around you." Then she told me to lift my hair. "Now sit down. Thank you very much for doing that. It's necessary."

She rang the Tibetan bell once again, and I listened to it reverberate in the room. Just like before I felt a sense of spiritual calm wash over me. I wanted Mark to cross over to where he belonged, and I had the feeling that Lily would be able to help him.

"I'm supposed to acknowledge your courage and your bravery," she said, pausing momentarily. "All I need you to do is say his name three times."

"Mark," I said three times.

"He hears you," Lily said. "Something about your voice is very soothing to him. He just wants to listen to your heart. He's just hearing your heart. The reason why his soul is kind of on hold is because . . . hearing your heart isn't necessarily all the lovey-dovey stuff. It's a way for him to take responsibility for his choices and his actions. Hearing your heart means to be able to express from the core of your being all that you have felt and experienced up to this time. Hearing your heart is also a way for your heart to release and to feel at peace. It doesn't matter what anyone else's opinions and thoughts are that are negative. Everybody has an opinion. They're like belly buttons. You must listen to your own heart in regards to him. It's almost like when a child does something they aren't supposed to do, and a good parent will intercede and tell them why they shouldn't have done that. And this is almost like hearing your heart. The kindness that you have shown him is excruciating for his soul because he can't accept it, because he feels as though he has violated something so sacred, so beautiful, and so pure that his soul—Okay, I have to stop because he's right here. What the heck happened to him? What happened, sweetheart?"

"He lost sight of that love for a second when his family was gone, and he took his own life," I said. "He couldn't see past the depression and some bad choices that he made, and he left. He just left. He didn't reach out. He didn't give us time to help him. He just—"

"Let me explain something to you. Didn't you notice . . . didn't it feel like almost a *Dr. Jekyll and Mr. Hyde* thing going on? Didn't you notice that? Let me explain what this is. I don't know what was in his system. I don't know if it was antidepressants. I don't know if it was alcohol. I don't know what it was. But there are these things.

They are lower-frequency entities. They are like cockroaches, and they are all around us."

"Is he here?" I asked.

"Yes, he's right here. When you said his name, all I could see was a big smile. He asked me if I could see him and hear him, and I said I could. I feel like he doesn't even know what happened to him. I'll tell you what happened to him. One of those things I told you about took over and said, 'Let's destroy this family. Let's destroy this family's self-esteem. Let's destroy this family's honor. Because then if we do this, it's going to have an effect on generations to come.' Guess what those identities feed on? Depression, sadness, fear, and failure. And he's on the other side, crying and wondering what happened. Let me tell you—you can shift that quickly, so that's why I smudged you down. I wanted to see if anything had attached itself to you. I am going to send you home with something that will clear your environment."

"I keep losing weight," I said. "I can't—"

"It wants to feed off you."

"Yes," I said. "I hate it."

"The thing is," she said, "it will feed off the sadness, the sorrow, the depression. It will feed off the lack of self-esteem. It will feed off all that shit. He's stuck in limbo because he doesn't know what the fuck happened." Lily paused. "I'm sorry I have to talk that way."

"That's all right," I said.

"He's like, 'What the hell happened?'"

"I say that all the time," I said, crying. "What happened?"

"This is where an entity comes in and wants to destroy. I've seen it happen many times. In fact, it's what I'm writing about. That's so ironic."

She wanted to pause for a moment, and she told Mark to stay where he was. Then she told me she was writing a story about a woman who didn't know who her husband was because he was a totally different person. Her friends told her it was because he had died, but then she realized that he wasn't her husband anymore.

Lily went on to explain that physically it had been Mark who had crossed over. "My head hurts," she said suddenly.

"Mine too."

"This is one of those things that feeds off thoughts," she said. "That's why it feels like it hurts too much. How did he kill himself, sweetheart?"

"He killed himself in my car," I said, "and I smell carbon monoxide."

"You do?" she asked.

"It's in my house too."

"That's because he hasn't crossed over. Let me talk to him some more. Say his name for me once more."

I began to repeat Mark's full name.

"He's smiling," Lily said. "Oh, my God. He's smiling."

Mark began to pace back and forth, not wanting to be where he was. I knew that and felt frustrated. I wanted to help him so much. But just knowing that Lily understood how I felt, just being around her was making me feel calmer than I had since Mark's death.

"He doesn't want to be where he is."

"I know he doesn't," I said.

"He feels like he's been watching something through a glass. And no matter how hard he hit the glass or pushed the glass, it was impossible for him to get any message through. To him it almost feels like he's in some sort of bubble. He says that his mind has been thinking and thinking about the sequence of events that happened prior to his crossing over."

"Yes," I said. "We named it 'the perfect storm.'"

"He said it felt mechanical like a zombie walking out the door. He felt that it wasn't him doing it."

"Yes!" I interrupted.

"It was almost like a voice telling him he had no other choice, any other way out. It was almost like it wasn't his body moving, like being in a dream. Then he realized it wasn't a dream."

CHAPTER 13

"He realized that he wasn't in his physical body anymore when his body was discovered," Lily continued.

"That was twenty-five hours later," I said.

"It was almost like he woke up and was watching everything and thought, *What's that?* It was terrifying for him. Oh, my God! Oh, my God! It's like his soul was trying to get back in, but he couldn't. The energy almost felt like being sucked through a tunnel, but it's not. Then everything turned gray. Where there was color, there is no color. It's almost like he's been watching . . . following. Let me explain to you where he's at. He's a ghost."

"I know," I said. "I know."

"I'm talking to him, and I'm telling him he has a choice. He can either stay in the gray space, or he can move on. He feels that if he hangs around, he can still be—"

"A part of our lives," I interrupted.

"He must have watched that movie *Ghost*," Lily said.

"It was one of our favorites," I said.

"That's what it is. That's why he's staying where he is."

"I just talked about it," I said.

"'I want to tell her I love her,'" Lily said, conveying Mark's message. "'I want to tell her I'm confused and don't understand.'"

She began to speak to Mark. "Here's the choice. You could sit in between." She paused, and I knew she was listening to Mark. "Okay." She turned to me. "I have to ask you this. He has a fear that if he's already dead and it's as gray as where he is now, that if he goes forward, he's going to go to even a worse place. I'm telling him he's not going to a worse place. It's called 'the healing place.' It's a place where he will be surrounded by the most beautiful, unconditional love. It's a place for your soul to heal." She began to address Mark. "The only way to get rid of the entity that has invaded your home, your safe space, is for you to make that transition over. That's the only way you can heal. You'll be able to visit them as often as you like if you go toward that space. See it?"

I listened in amazement as Lily spoke to Mark as though he were right there in the room with us. He was as real to her as I was—in a sense, as alive as I was . . . only in another form. Slowly I felt a sense of peace enter my body. I wanted the same for Mark.

"It's very small," Lily said. "He says he can't fit. He's asking me how he's going to fit, and I keep telling him he doesn't have to fit. All you have to do is allow it to come toward you and trust that you're not going to be punished for what you did."

"He was a beautiful person," I said, "a beautiful soul."

"You need to remember that you're not going to be punished for whatever you did," Lily told him. "The light's getting bigger. The light's getting much, much bigger. He's looking at his hands. Oh, it's so beautiful."

I gasped softly.

"His skin is turning gold. You'll be able to go, and you'll be able to see her. And you can go into her dreams better. She'll feel better. It's up to his shoulders now. This is good. He's starting to giggle. He says it tickles and feels like bubbles. Now comes all the memories, the memories of the children and holding them for the first time."

"Yes," I said softly. I was filled with so much emotion that it was almost unbearable.

"He remembers seeing them for the first time and the laughter and the silliness. There's an older woman who's coming forward. She's like a mother-grandmother figure."

I could barely speak. "Yes."

"He's asking me if he can go," Lily said. "Yes, you can't stay in the space you're in now."

"Yes," I said, "go. Go!"

"He's saying he can't hold this space much longer. He's almost all the way in." Lily kept telling him to go into the light. "She's got him!" Lily cried. "Oh, my God! There are more people. There's a lot of people around him. He's so beautiful! Oh, my God!" Lily repeated. "That space is closed. Let them love you," she said to Mark.

"Like we did," I said.

Lily continued to talk to Mark, saying, "Remember all the good stuff. Remember it. I have to go into your house now, sweetheart. This part is not going to be the easiest part, so let me follow where this is leading. In this life we must coexist with things that take innocent lives. I see what it is. It reminds me of a female succubus. It's a demon—whatever you want to call it—but it's female. It feeds so it can create sexual addictions. It will affect self-esteem. It will affect sexuality.

"I see her. She's right in the corner. You can't stay here anymore. You have to go. I've got her out. The older female is here—the one who grabbed your husband into her arms. She told me to tell you that he'll be okay now. She's keeping her eyes on the kids to remind them of the good things that happened, the good things they experienced with their father. She's so proud of them. It's been really hard for them to talk to their friends about what happened. One of them feels very unlovable, like he lost his very best friend."

"Cory," I said.

"He's going to need a little extra attention," Lily said. "You need to help him get through the hard parts, but he'll be fine. I need you to do three things. The main cockroach was called a succubus. They can come out of a porn site. They can come out of a bar. They can be sitting and waiting. They can jump off of someone. Any alcohol needs to be removed from the house. Get new stuff if you have to. Just remove any alcohol and any old prescriptions that he might have had."

"I got some of it out," I said.

"Good."

"But he had stuff stored in the basement that's still there," I added.

"Get rid of it," Lily said. "Anything that's alcohol, get rid of it. I need you to take regular salt and just go around the perimeter of the house. And as you're going around the house, you're just going to keep saying, 'This house is blessed with peace and joy and happiness.'"

"There are three places," I said. "Do you mean all of them?"

"You have to put salt either in the corners or around all of them," Lily answered. "I found the cockroaches under the bed. It's almost as if the things that came with the succubus wait for your kids to sleep and then give them nightmares and all kinds of crap."

I thought of the nightmares Eva and I had both had.

"The next thing you're going to do—and this is going to sound a little goofy—you're going to need to put a little water, seven drops of lavender oil, and three drops of tea tree oil under each of the beds. What that does is creates a space that says, 'Don't come here because if you come here, you're going to have to go.' Basically you had an infestation that took a life, and now you're saying, 'No more.' Right now there's a bond of angelic beings around your house. They are like swords of protection around your house. They are actually clearing your house right now. You have to do these other things just to be safe, and then I want you to play healing, angelic music nonstop. You need to do this for at least three days. So you have a lot to do, but you can get all the items at a health food store. It's not expensive, but it's worth it."

Regardless of the cost, I knew I didn't want to continue on as we had. The pain, both physical and emotional, had almost cost me my life and the well-being of my children. I listened more closely as Lily continued to speak, not wanting to miss a word she said.

"You need to drink a lot of water during the next three days—no alcohol. No one is to have any alcohol! You can't have any alcohol in your home for two weeks because if it's going to come back, it will come through the alcohol. Now I have to ask you—Did your husband drink?"

"Sure. Not every day, but drinking was a factor."

"That was how it got in," Lily replied. "It would not have gotten in if he hadn't been drinking. I've seen this with my own son. I've seen this with hundreds of people in other parts of the country. It can hook on in a public, social place. He could have been at a bar, and it could have been there and attached itself to him—like that! It will look for that weakest moment, and then it just takes over. It slowly seeps in. It actually becomes like a leech. What it's trying to do is break you down."

"I know," I said.

"That's why you're nice and thin," she said with a laugh. "I'd love to be nice and thin, but as you can see, it's not my thing."

"This is not intentional," I said.

"Right. It's sucking off your energy. But there's nothing attached to you, so it's doing it at night. Your husband is going to come to you in a dream. I don't know when it will be. But when he does, he's going to be smiling because when he crossed, he *was* smiling. When I was talking to you about *Ghost*, he was telling me that he saw that movie, and I told him there are other ways that you can communicate."

"He's done that," I said. "He's moved things, and he's found things."

"Yes, but he felt that he was stuck. He couldn't move. He couldn't go anywhere."

"My daughter made the bed you saw for him in a dream," I said.

"Really? How beautiful. That was his safe space."

"He couldn't stand anymore," I said, "so that's why she made it for him."

Lily was obviously moved by Eva's loving gesture. "He was so grateful for that. He really was. To leave that space was hard for him, but now he's in the arms of people who really love him. Memories are going to come up. This is what happens. They are going to come with emotions, tears, laughter, silliness. You're going to think that he's responding to you. Let the emotions flow. Do not put yourself on antidepressants. If you do that, it will stop the healing process. I just need you to flow with it. If people ask you if you're okay, just tell them you're having a moment. He'll start talking to you. He'll start talking to you much clearer. The last thing he ever wanted to do was hurt his loved ones, his family.

"Everyone has opinions, but the one thing you know is that the core of your relationship has always been love. You have him close to your heart always, and he knows that. He listens to your heart. That's what I see in regards to him. Now the last thing you're going to do is—and I want you to do this with your children, even though they might think it's a little hokey. How old are your children?"

"Twenty-three, twenty-one, and seventeen," I answered.

"I want you to tell them you're going to do something very special. Are they close?"

"One's in California, but the other two are."

"Do it in California," Lily said. "Everybody has to have one white candle, and then just have them light the candle with love. They should tell their father that they love him and that they're happy he's on the other side now. Usually the seven-day candles are good. Keep them lit until they burn out. They should be in a safe space. They may not be happy with the way this turned out, but the energy of true love never ceases to exist. It continues to grow and get stronger. He does love you very, very, very, very much, but something happened that he didn't love himself. Something convinced him, and I can't even explain it. It's almost like putting on a Halloween costume, and you have another exterior, but that's not who you are in your heart. That's where the other shit comes in, that crap that I've seen since I was a baby. Now do you have questions for me, baby girl? Because I'm going to ring the bell again and look at you and tell you some things that might be in your path, okay?"

Once again I heard the bell and listened to the sound.

"I see you very clearly," Lily began. "The reason you're having difficulty and you're losing weight is because this was very hard for your soul to digest. It was contrary to your soul's vision, your vision of what love is supposed to be—that you and your husband would grow old together and that everything would be wonderful."

"He lost sight," I said.

"It was the thing," Lily said. "He's taken responsibility for allowing it to enter, but it was the thing. You're a cobra, and your cobra is kind of at the starting line. It's saying, 'All you have to do is give me an okay.' Spiritually there's a part of you that's ready. It's almost like the two of you went so far that your souls have been entwined for many lifetimes. This is not the first lifetime you've had together."

"I knew that when I saw him the first time."

"The last thing he ever wanted to do was feel like a failure, but taking all the good before the *Dr. Jekyll and Mr. Hyde* thing happened. What I want you to do is understand that you're at this new starting point. Part of you didn't want that. It wasn't in your soul contract. But there's a high probability that you will fall in love again. One of the things that will be important is to build trust. So remember that if any opportunities come along, you make the choice. You could spend your life alone because he was who you loved."

"He was my person," I said.

"But there is a possibility that someone else will come in to assist you in healing part of your heart. When you are ready, okay?"

"Yes," I said.

"I'm going to suggest that you look for things that uplift you. If you enjoy going to plays, then go to plays. If you love to hear your children laugh, then listen to their laughter. You are going to notice that you're very sensitive to sound and the things that people say. So when you're ready to go forward, then you're ready to go forward. Through this process you have learned who your real friends are. Some people just wanted to know the dirty details, and they had opinions. You also learned who you could trust.

"We're all going to die, whether we die in an accident or whether we are murdered, but we're going to die. Don't let anyone judge you. Let me tell you something. No one could have loved him and supported him as deeply as you did as his wife, as his companion, as co-parents—no one. His soul knows that. That's why he was sitting on that cot. Let me tell you. On the other side there are all kinds of women, but all he cared about was you. When you see *Ghost* the next time, that's going to be him looking at you. And he was concerned because he didn't know what to do. He was trapped and didn't know what to do."

"I could feel that," I said.

"You're going to get more messages, but don't be afraid, because they are coming from a higher plane. If your TV turns itself on or you hear a song that belonged to the two of you or something falls, smile and say, 'Thanks for being here.' Now he's a spirit, not a ghost. We are all spirits. But he got to the ghost part, and that's not a good place."

We listened a moment as her grandson cried upstairs.

"You need to remember the good things he did in life. Just because this bad choice was made doesn't disqualify everything you did that was right and true. *If I had done this* or *I should have done that*—don't do that to yourself, because that's what will draw those things in, and they will feed off it. You could have been in the house in the next room, and when that thing was ready to take it, it would take it. That would have been worse."

CHAPTER 14

"The next thing is . . . you should tell your story to people," Lily said. "Some people aren't going to believe you. I can't tell you how many times I've done this, but I can tell you that many people's lives have been changed. Some of these things attach when they are little, and some attach when they are older. And they feed off fear and failure. You are surrounded by lots of angels because when I was smudging you I kept seeing all these halos, which means you're protected. People have been praying for you. You have good people around you. If you speak about what's happened to you, it will help others get through the process. But I can see in the throat chakra that sometimes you don't want to talk about it. Don't be afraid that you're talking about it too much. How many years were you married?"

"We were married twenty-five years and together twenty-nine."

"When did he cross over?"

"When he died?"

"Yes."

"April 13th," I answered. "And you knew that in Montpelier. And no one knew that because we didn't find him until the next day."

"I don't remember saying that," Lily said.

"I know. But that's what Robin said, and you wouldn't have had any way to know that."

"People think I sit down and do research," Lily said, "but I don't. My information comes from the other side. He didn't try to possess me either."

"He wasn't a bad person," I said.

"I like him," Lily said. "I don't think he was bad at all, but he was stuck. Now here's the next thing. In the heart chakra you are very good at putting things where they need to be. Do you know what I mean? So it's almost like these file cabinets of memories in your heart chakra—some of them look like treasure boxes. I'm going to tell you something. Should we recycle a thought over and over again? Do we tell our kids that we remember when they were three years old and they puked all over themselves? The heart chakra keeps saying that this terrible thing happened. It is what it is. Usually when souls are this close, when one goes, the other will go soon after, and maybe that's what this thing wanted."

"Well, I don't know," I said. "The thoughts were there. I just kept pushing them back."

"That's your strength," Lily said. "That's good, because you need to be here, sweetheart. There are grandchildren and great-grandchildren and all kinds of stuff for you to enjoy. You will love deeper. You will be more appreciative of the people around you, and you will make more time for the things that are important to you. Your vibration is much, much higher than the average person's because you aren't going to take anything for granted. When you're ready—because you don't want to do anything that tarnishes the love between you and your husband—individuals will come into your life. And you don't have to commit your life to them. You don't even have to have sex with them. But just allow yourself the possibility.

"I think you need to be comforted sometimes because you are so good at comforting others. The biggest problem you have is in your solar plexus, which is why you are losing a lot of weight. I need you to put your hand on your solar plexus at least once a day and rock yourself like a baby. It's almost like your solar plexus is like a colicky baby and it just needs to be held. Tell yourself you just need to eat and that if you eat something, you're going to feel better.

"Right now your passion is your children. Taking time with each one of your children, one-on-one, is a gesture of love and very important right now. They don't know what to say to you sometimes. They don't know how to approach you. Just look at them and love them and ask them how they're feeling without judgment. They are worried about you."

"I know they are," I said.

"They don't want you to be alone. I can see it."

"They witnessed our life," I replied, "and they knew what we meant to each other."

"All I'm going to say," Lily said, "is that without a shadow of a doubt there are forces around us, and we coexist. Where there is dark, there is light, and your soul has now experienced the light and the dark. And now your soul says, 'I need to be clear.'"

Spellbound in my chair, I continued to listen raptly.

"If it's a cockroach," Lily said, "it's a cockroach. They may live in the world, but I don't want them in my house."

I had the feeling that I knew what she was talking about, but I wanted to hear it from her.

"Somehow this thing got into your house," she explained. "Usually the average person doesn't know it's a cockroach—that's what I call these things. There are people who will take advantage of people who have cockroaches. Your love, your faith in what your relationship really was, your love for each other and your children, and even all that you lost is what will sustain your soul through time and all eternity. If the soul stays focused on what was traumatic and tragic, then the soul will remain stuck. So what I would say to you is, 'Talk to him.'

"Now you are going to see signs. In fact, you already have. You're going to see birds looking at you and butterflies and all kinds of things. Just smile. You're going to feel alone, but I want you to know something. He must have loved you so deeply that he's not going anywhere."

"That's why I had to come," I said.

"And then to come all the way to Montpelier to see me," Lily said. "That's wild. This isn't the first time this has happened. It's happened before, and the person who was supposed to hear it wasn't even there. You need to replenish yourself. What was it that he would say to you that would always make you smile and feel good?"

"One thing?" I asked. "He always called me Hoke. And his hugs. He said he loved me every day. I know how much he loved me."

"No one is prepared for death," Lily said. "Not even if someone is terminally ill. Yesterday I asked a friend if she was ever afraid of dying because one way or another we're going to die. But it's how we live our lives, no matter how we die. That's what matters. How he lived his life is what matters, not how he died. I have to tell you that he looks totally different now. He's right behind you on your heart side, which is where he should be. He's dressed very nicely. He's a handsome man—very, very handsome. He's smiling—"

"He had a huge smile," I said.

"He wants me to tell you that he just met two of your grandchildren who will be coming into the family. He's thrilled because he never thought he would have the opportunity to meet his grandchildren before they were actually born. So when the children come, he will be escorting them into the home. And they might have little bits and pieces of his personality, so be prepared for that—something to look forward to. He wants you to know that there is always hope and that you are his hope. Never give up hope. He says he will see you soon. Someday if you're looking into the mirror and you think you see something happening on the side, it's probably him. 'I love you,' he says."

"I love you too," I said.

"He keeps kissing your face," Lily said. "He feels like a weight has been lifted from his shoulders, and he wishes he could just dance with you. If there was a song that was your favorite, put it on, close your eyes, and just let him dance with you. He's at peace. His soul is at peace. You will get a sign that he's at peace. Just keep your eyes open. He told me to tell you, 'Thank you.'"

"I didn't want to do this at first," I confessed. "I was going to have to do something beyond losing him, but it's okay. I knew I had to come."

Chapter 15

fter the session with Lily my sister-in-law drove me to West Castleton. I was exhausted and sweaty but jazzed. I had never given much credence to mediums. Certainly Mark never had. But I felt physically and emotionally bowled over by the experience. Even now words fail.

Ann and I drove to my mother's apartment in West Castleton, a small town about forty-five miles southwest of Montpelier. She lived in a comfortable two-bedroom apartment on the second floor of a charming yellow and white seniors' complex. The apartment featured an adjoining living room and kitchen plus a small dining area with a round dining room table, which was always covered with a pretty tablecloth. Mom had adorned her home with antiques, treasures she would someday pass on to her children.

Crippled by osteoporosis, my mother walked with the aid of a walker. At one time she had stood five feet ten inches tall, but she would shrink to five-foot-one by the end. Although hampered physically, she still had a sharp mind and a sassy sense of humor. She wore her gray hair short and boasted a contagious laugh. Her faded brown eyes only hinted at her talent for sarcasm. She never failed to get the best of me, leaving me to wonder afterward how she'd managed to figure me out and make light of her insights at the same time. I often wanted to be mad at her, but I knew that was impossible.

My mom asked about my session with Lily, and I told her that it had helped me a great deal. But I didn't talk much about it. I was too busy mulling over everything Lily had instructed me to do. In any case Mom mostly just wanted to know if I was all right. *Everybody*, especially my kids, wanted to know if I was okay. Ann's husband, Kevin, picked her up and took her home, leaving me to stay overnight with Mom.

We went to bed early that night because I was so tired I could hardly keep my eyes open. But I only slept for a short time and then woke up. As I lay on my back in bed, I felt the strangest sensation. It was as if someone was pulling a part of my energy—my soul—from my body and just unraveling it through my feet. Suddenly I felt super energized and happy like I could do anything. I got up and scrubbed my mom's kitchen floor and her refrigerator. Next I cleaned out some cabinets, including an antique cabinet that was stuffed with junk my mother had been unwilling to part with.

When she woke up at six the next morning, I was still puttering around the apartment.

"What's going on?" she asked.

"I don't know," I answered. "I just can't help it. I feel like everything that's been wrong with me—all the bad stuff—was pulled out. It's gone."

I guess you could say that a weight had been lifted from my shoulders, but that old cliché hardly described how incredible I felt. Maybe Mark wasn't living as a ghost anymore and therefore was no longer living off my energy and depleting it. Maybe my energy was being refueled and renewed. Whatever had happened, I felt positively liberated.

I said good-bye to my mom and drove to the farm to visit Lizzy for a little while, and after that I went back to the lake and called the kids, telling them I had work to do and they were welcome to join me there if they wanted. Lily had said that my spaces had to be cleared of the bad entities. Many who died by suicide didn't act alone but were assisted by the cockroaches, themselves addicts when they had been alive. The cockroaches still thrived on those addictions, which was why they would attach themselves to someone in a bar. They thrived on taking people with them. That part of what Lily had told me had surprised and frightened me. Now all I wanted to do was clear my spaces and begin the healing process.

We had all been having such disturbing dreams and nightmares, not just about Mark. I had chalked them up to stress. But Lily had told me how to put solutions—I called them bad dream catchers—under the bed to keep those entities from visiting us in our dreams and trying to alter our thinking. I decided to follow her instructions and clear all of our spaces, even the lake house, although we weren't sleeping there at the time. I was to take a type of incense made from a combination of sage and a few other ingredients and burn it in a bowl. Next I was to light the polo santo stick, a wood from South America used to clear bad spirits, and then smudge myself and the environment. As I did that, I was to repeat a simple incantation: "Joy, love, and peace reside in this place, and you are not welcome here."

Of course I felt self-conscious throughout the rituals, including the one that required me to pour a circle of salt around the house. When Eva and Cory arrived at the lake house, I smudged them before they could enter, and they rolled their eyes in protest. But they jumped right in and helped me clear the house of alcohol and Mark's old prescription drugs. We found cases and cases of Canadian beer Mark had stored in the basement, took them outside, and poured them into the snow. It was a time-consuming process, but I felt energized throughout.

After we finished with the lake house, the kids decided they'd had enough and returned to the apartment in Burlington. But I still had the cottage to purify. Unfortunately when I tried to unlock the door, the key wouldn't work on the lock. I tried repeatedly but couldn't get the door to unlock. I thought about what Lily had said about cockroaches and remembered the snowstorm that had almost prevented me from visiting her. Was someone or something trying to keep me from clearing the space in the cottage, the very place where Mark had died? Something bad was there. I could feel it.

I drove back to the apartment in Burlington and repeated the rituals. Then we called Charlie in San Francisco, and we each lit a white candle to show Mark that we still remembered him, still loved him, and were glad he was in a good place. Lily had instructed me to burn lemongrass, but I had found a diffuser and put lemongrass oil in the diffuser to cleanse the apartment. She had also told me to avoid alcohol for a couple weeks and to play uplifting music. Not surprisingly her recommendations made me feel better. I felt more in control of my emotions—maybe not totally in control but more so than I'd been in months.

It had been quite a three-day weekend. When Monday morning rolled around, my friends at work noticed a definite improvement the minute I walked into the office. The grief lines on my face had softened. I was smiling more, glowing even. I had a skip in my step. Aaron, whom I had continued to see regularly and who had been instrumental in helping me survive, noticed the changes as well, telling me I looked different, healthier, and less stressed. The kids, too, saw the difference. I'd only told a few people about the rituals. But those who knew—my kids, Tom, and Sue—gave me their full support. They were certainly skeptical, but I don't think anyone was going to debate the results.

About a month later I finally returned to the cottage with Sue. This time around we had no problem getting inside. I have no idea why I'd been unable to unlock the door the first time. We performed the rituals, dumped all the alcohol and medication, including cold medication, and put bad dream catchers under every bed. The latter ritual had already had a positive impact on us back at the apartment, where even Cory admitted he'd had more pleasant dreams of late.

Lily had linked Mark's death from carbon monoxide poisoning to the headaches I'd been experiencing, which came on whenever his spirit was near. Sure enough, my headaches had disappeared since his crossing over. Following Lily's recommendations, I'd stopped taking my medications as well. As a result I felt less stressed. I felt lighter.

CHAPTER 16

hen February arrived, I realized I had a decision to make. My gut was telling me it was time for a change of scenery. But my head was telling me to stay put so Cory could finish out the remainder of high school at the same Catholic school in Burlington, hanging out with the same friends and doing the same things he'd done before Mark's death. It wasn't an easy decision to make. I was feeling stronger every day. I was healing. But along with the rest of my family, I still had a long way to go.

After I considered my options, I went with my head, although not without reservations. I would wait until Cory graduated the following year before I pulled up stakes and started looking for a new home. For now we would try to maintain our routine. I had been going to Cory's high school hockey games all season and tried to be as supportive as possible. Aaron had often traveled with me to the games, offering moral support, and as the season had progressed, I'd grown braver and had started going with other people. Cory had one last regular-season game scheduled for the following day, and I asked an old high school friend to come with me to watch him play. She readily agreed. She wanted to hear about my session with Lily and suggested we meet for an early dinner before we went to the hockey game.

On the day of the regular season finale, Eva came home from school to lend her voice to our little cheering section. We hadn't been watching the game for long when Cory took a bad hit against the boards and fell awkwardly to the ice. We traded nervous glances as he hobbled off the ice and took a seat on the bench. We didn't think too much of it until he got back on the ice for his next shift and fell right into the boards again. When he tried to retake his feet, he fell again. He finally skated a short distance toward the boards, and the team doctor and the trainer escorted him to the examination table, which was adjacent to the bench.

Oh, no, I thought. *This can't be good.*

From our vantage point in the stands, it looked like the problem was his right knee. Then I saw the doctor's wife, who knew me, start to walk toward us. I hurried to the examination table, and by that time another doctor, an orthopedist, was examining Cory.

"His ACL is gone," he said. "He's torn it. He won't be able to suit up for the playoffs. He's going to need surgery."

I returned to the stands and told Eva what was going on while they iced his knee and found him a pair of crutches. After I located someone who could help me bring his car home, I met Cory near the ice. He was devastated, and we both broke down in tears. Just when we'd thought things were starting to get better, we'd been dealt another vicious blow. In that moment I realized I'd made a bad decision to stay put the day before. I hadn't felt right about it then, and now I knew it had been the wrong choice. I needed to listen to my instincts.

With his driving leg out of commission, Cory would be unable to get around on his own. He would have to walk on crutches at school. And he would need surgery in five weeks. In the meantime we lived in a second-story apartment without an elevator. This was a kid who'd already suffered one of the most terrible blows imaginable in losing his father—and now this. Like Mark, Cory constantly battled depression, anxiety, and anger, even during good times, and he was awfully good at taking out his frustrations on me. I didn't know how either one of us was going to cope with this latest calamity.

Perhaps not surprisingly Norma resurfaced later that night, and I took off in the dark. The roads were slushy. Visibility was lousy. But I found my way to the lake house. After I parked my car, I marched out onto the ice and waited, hoping the ice would be too thin to hold my weight, praying I'd fall through. Worried about Cory's injury, not sure what to do about the lake house, devastated that we couldn't heal, I was ready to give up. But the ice held. When I realized I wasn't going anywhere, I sulked off the ice and sat down on Mark's beach chair, which stayed on the beach all winter. I started talking to Mark and asking God for help—something I hadn't done much of since Mark's death. It was a start. Somehow I needed to find the will to live.

I never went inside the lake house that night. I just sat on the beach and talked. After a while I didn't feel like hurting myself. I went back to the apartment, and Norma disappeared.

Cory went in for knee surgery at the beginning of March, but he didn't tolerate the procedure well. He had to have the incision drained twice, ran a fever most of the time, and stayed on pain meds longer than the doctors recommended. Angry and depressed, he needed a while to withdraw from the medication and was ill during most of that time. It took him two weeks to get back to school. Six weeks would pass before he began to feel like himself again.

The abuse he unleashed on me left me wondering why we couldn't get a break. Cory, adopting a poor-me attitude, was angry that he had lost his dad . . . and angry with me because I was there and his father wasn't. He didn't want to talk about it much. But when he did, he had terrible meltdowns. By the end of March he asked me why we were still living in Burlington.

"What do you mean?" I asked.

"I want to get out of here," he said. "I don't want to go to school here anymore. I can't live here anymore. I can't play hockey, and I don't *want* to play hockey. I need a different life."

"Do you want to move?" I asked.

"Yes," he said.

My head was spinning. How could I make that happen? How could I possibly give him a new life and move out of an area I had lived in for thirty years? I would have to quit a job I loved but wasn't really performing well at anymore, and I would have to sell my dream house that I had built with Mark but had come to hate and wished would burn to the ground. I didn't want the house anymore, but I didn't know how to let go of it. I didn't know if I had the emotional stability or physical strength to pack up two places and move my daughter again for her senior year of college—all at the same time. My lease was going to be up in the apartment, so that wasn't going to be a problem. But where to start with the lake house?

I instantly thought of Wade, a former lake neighbor who had shown interest in the lake house. About six feet two inches tall, slim, and good-looking, he was in his mid to late forties. He had a big white smile and was in excellent shape. He was always on the move, always changing things, always full of energy. A self-made millionaire and owner of several successful businesses, he had once owned a piece of property just two lots down from ours on the lake. After he had bought the property, he had ignored the local laws and built a huge log home on the lot, taking advantage of several people on the lake in the process. And during his time on the lake he had kept to himself and hadn't socialized much with the group of neighbors who lived along the shoreline. We'd rarely seen him, except when he was barreling down the roads like a military recruit at boot camp. Thus, he had earned a reputation as someone who used people—and his property—for his gain only. He eventually sold his property to a celebrity. But he still visited the property on occasion to look after it when it wasn't being used.

Wade missed being on the lake and had expressed interest in buying the lake house after Mark's death. I called him and told him I was thinking of selling it.

"If you're going to list it," he said, "put me as an exclusion."

Doing so would give him the inside track to buying the property, and I agreed to the suggestion, although not without some reservations. I was wary of dealing with a man whose reputation was sleazy at best.

After I listed the house, I decided to start the search for a place to live in southern Vermont. I promised Cory that if we moved, we would live in a house, not an apartment or duplex. We would live in a place where we could feel like a family again, a place where we could celebrate the holidays together, a place close to a decent school district.

I was worried he had made the decision to move under duress. He wasn't in a good place, and I didn't know whether or not to believe that he was serious. All I knew was that I wanted to leave . . . badly. I didn't want to live Mark's life. I hated the way I felt. At work I felt like there was a big sign on my back that read, *My husband killed himself.* People would whisper behind my back, or they would look at me with pity in their eyes. My friends had changed. When they called, they wanted to know what I needed, not how I was. They no longer wanted to make plans or go out and do fun things together. The lone exception was Aaron, but most of the time we talked about Mark's death. When he would try to reengage me in life with other people, I would turn him down because I no longer had those skills.

I forged ahead and started to make appointments to look at houses in southern Vermont. I checked websites and newspapers. Could I make this work? I began driving down to southern Vermont every weekend, looking for a house to rent and spending the rest of my free time packing up the lake house, going through all of Mark's things, and taking some of it to Goodwill. That was probably one of the most difficult things to do—having to sort through it all. Some of the stuff I could part with, but most of it I couldn't. I eventually boxed up much of it.

On Easter weekend I checked out a handful of rentals but was disappointed by what I found. The homes were expensive, not very nice, and located in neighborhoods that didn't meet my standards. I couldn't help feeling discouraged.

"It's not looking good," I told Cory. "It's hard to find a house that's in decent shape, in a good school district, and doesn't cost a fortune."

I also wanted to be on the west side so we would be close enough to visit my mother, who was now living in an assisted living facility in West Castleton. She had suffered a mild stroke back in November and had been put in a nursing home in January to recover. I wanted to spend more time with her before her final sunset. As it turned out, she would live just one more year, and she would spend eight months of her final year bedridden.

Discouraged, I spent Easter weekend at Lizzy's farm with Eva and Cory. Eva went back to school on Easter Sunday, but Cory and I stayed the night. Before I left with Cory on Monday, I looked through the want ads in the Sunday newspaper and found a couple of rental homes that appeared to be worth visiting on our way home. One of the houses was perfectly located in Middleburg, but I was certain there was no way I could afford it.

The first house we looked at was located in the Sun Valley Area School District, not far from where my twin brother, Keith, lived, so I was hopeful. Those hopes were quickly dashed the moment we got out of the car. The house sat on an overgrown lot and was filthy inside. The previous tenants had stolen the refrigerator, and there was actually a dead mouse in a light socket. Despite all this, the rent was through the roof.

Cory and I left, disgusted.

"Find that ad in the newspaper for the Middleburg house," I said. "What can it hurt to call?"

Cory found the ad, and I dialed the number.

A gentleman by the name of Ryan answered after a few rings.

"Is the house still for rent?" I asked.

"Yes," he answered. "It's being repaired right now, and there's a lot of work being done. Let me tell you what happened—"

He proceeded to tell me about pipes that had frozen the previous winter, causing about $50,000 worth of damage. He was in the middle of making the necessary repairs.

"The real estate market is soft," he said, "so I'm not looking to sell it. But I *am* looking to rent it. But I don't want a big family to live in it. I would prefer not so many people."

Ryan asked me what my story was, and I told him it would be just me and my son moving down from Burlington. "I'm looking for a house to rent," I said, "and I want to be in a certain school district. Middleburg fits my criteria, but there's no way I can pay the rent you're asking for."

"Well, just come and look at it. Make it the first house you look at when you're here next weekend."

"I'll be here next Friday," I said.

"Well, make my house the first one."

I set up an appointment for 11:00 a.m. and later arranged to look at two other homes.

When I went back on Friday, I took Lizzy and Ann, my sister-in-law, since she was in property management.

Ryan opened the door and immediately recognized Ann. He was the same age as me, of average build, and not especially attractive. I found him intimidating.

The house though was beautiful despite all the repairs going on. At four thousand square feet it would easily accommodate us. It had three bedrooms, a loft area, two and a half bathrooms, a large kitchen, a dining room, a screened porch, and a workout room in the basement. It wasn't an apartment, duplex, or condo; it was a home. It was perfect. I could already envision where my furniture would go, which was a relief. I wouldn't have to sell anything or put things in storage; I could just bring my life down there and not have to part with anything before I was ready. The neighborhood, too, was just right: upscale, on the west side of Montpelier, reasonably close to West Castleton, and located in a good school district.

After Ryan showed us around, he asked me to make him an offer.

I got all flustered. "Let me think about it," I said.

We got back into the car, and Ann told me she wasn't a fan of Ryan.

"He's a hard-ass," she said. "He doesn't treat his employees very well. Be careful."

Unfortunately the other two houses we looked at that day paled in comparison to Ryan's rental. They were in bad locations and in poor shape.

I called Ryan from Ann's that night and made him an offer. He made a counteroffer, and after a bit of haggling we came to terms. Then he got in touch with one of his property managers from his rental company to get the ball rolling. A week later after I had completed all of the requisite paperwork, Cory and I had a place to live in southern Vermont.

Chapter 17

On the one-year anniversary of Mark's death just as Cory and I were finding a new home, I received a friend request on Facebook from Katherine, an old high school friend whose husband, also a former classmate, had passed away shortly before Mark. I'd heard through the grapevine that he had committed suicide. After I had learned of his death, I had looked through my old high school yearbook with Mark.

"It never gets this bad," I had told Mark at the time. "Just remember it never gets this bad."

Now more than a year later I couldn't remember what had made me say that. I'd known then that Mark was in a bad place, and I'd felt horribly distraught while I had looked at this old high school classmate's picture in the yearbook. Had I known what was coming? A month later he would be gone.

I was delighted to hear from Katherine and quickly accepted her request.

Thanks for reaching out to me on the anniversary of my husband's death, I wrote.

She e-mailed me back and wrote, *Oh, my God. I had no idea. We are going through the same thing at the exact same time.*

As Katherine and I continued to catch up with each other, she began to read through my Facebook posts. Shortly after my first visit with Lily, I had begun posting my reflections on a fairly regular basis.

One such post mentioned a dream I'd had while I'd been living in the apartment. In the dream I had noticed a bright light coming from my bedroom. At first I'd thought the light was coming from Eva, who was lying on the bed with her computer. But then I had realized it was coming from Mark, who was lying on the bed and basking in a golden light. Young and beautiful, he was smiling. I walked over and lay down beside him. He didn't speak, but I could hear his thoughts.

I'm sorry.

I know, I responded.

I love you.

I love you too.

We shared a hug and a laugh, and then the dream ended.

After she read through all my posts and realized that she and I were going through the same thing, Katherine told me she wasn't sure *why* she had contacted me in the first place. It was almost as if someone or something had physically taken her to the computer and made her send me the friend request.

What was Mark doing? What was happening?

After I agreed to Ryan's terms for the rental house in Middleburg, everything snowballed from there. Eva, Cory, and I began to pack up the lake house and the apartment. I gave notice at work, and we started showing the house. At first there wasn't much interest. But Wade, the gentleman who had told me to put him down as an exclusion, came by the lake house one weekend while I was packing our things. He was a pretty smooth businessman, but as he took a look around the place, I remembered how much my husband had disliked him. Although I tolerated him at best, I was feeling desperate. I wanted badly to get away from my in-laws and the lake, where I couldn't breathe. I hated the lake house and knew I could never live there again.

I felt like running as fast as I could to a new life. So when he offered me less money than I wanted, I agreed to sell the house to him. It felt *simple*. But something in my gut told me it wasn't right. We both signed a purchase agreement, and he included a clause stating that the agreement was good until July 15.

"No, no, no," I said. "I'm not doing this until July 15th. I'm going to be moving in June, and I'm not going to pay two rents."

"Oh, it will be done long before that," he assured me. "I'm just waiting on the sale of a property in Florida. And if it takes longer, I'll pay your house payment."

We packed up our lake house, hired movers, and moved into the house in Middleburg. Then after we moved out, Wade started to use my property for recreational purposes. He also cut my front woods down that were on the road side of the property because he didn't like them. He did all this before he had actually bought the house, before had he signed any papers, before he had given me a dime. I wasn't happy about what he had done, but I was too ill to fight him. The exhaustion of moving my daughter at college, packing up two places, and moving to Middleburg had reduced my five-foot-four frame to ninety-eight pounds, twenty-eight less than my weight the day Mark had died.

Cory, who was adding to my stress, then decided he hadn't really wanted to move. He was angry and depressed. He had no friends, no job, and a knee that still needed rehab. Meanwhile, Eva found a summer job at a camp and lasted all of two days before she quit and decided she couldn't be away from family. She hadn't expected to feel so isolated and lonely and was in a full-on panic.

"You can live here under one condition," I told her, "that you get a job immediately."

"That would be fine," she said.

Thus, the three of us were sitting in Middleburg in a house that we didn't know, looking at each other, wondering what we had done and how we were going to survive this.

I called Ryan, my landlord, and told him my daughter would be living there for the summer. I didn't think it would be a big deal, but he was furious.

"You're taking advantage of me," he scolded me. "You lied when you said only you and your son would be living there." He was angry, he told me, because there was going to be more wear and tear on the house.

I was in tears by the time I hung up. By the end of the summer I would pay six hundred dollars extra for Eva to stay there. It was clear that some people, people like Ryan, cared more about money than people. It was also clear that I wasn't healthy and couldn't handle anything beyond the stress of day-to-day living. I was likely suffering from post-traumatic stress disorder, and Cory's daily abuse didn't help. He yelled at me constantly, always threatening to go back to Burlington, saying he would live with a friend or his grandparents.

Eva was job hunting and felt like a total loser for bailing on the camp job, but I didn't know how to help her or her brother. I was in a bad place, questioning all the decisions I had made and watching everything slowly fall apart. I didn't know how to make it right for anybody. All I could do was take things one day at a time. I was still waiting to close on the lake house and tried to drive up there as often as possible to check on things, but I felt like Wade was taking advantage of me. I had no friends other than my family, and because I wasn't working, I was spending the most time of any of my siblings with my mom. Unfortunately visiting her simply added to the load I was carrying, which was already too burdensome.

It was hard for us to find our way that summer. Eva eventually landed a job as a waitress at a pub, and the decision to take the position paid off when she made some great contacts there. Maintaining a long-distance relationship with her boyfriend though was proving more onerous . . . and expensive. Cory, on the other hand, was spending most of his time sitting around and feeling sorry for himself. After Eva and I got on his case, he finally got out there and started looking for a job.

I was visiting Leah, my second oldest sister, after she'd had some minor surgery when I received a text message from Cory that he'd found a job at a pizza restaurant. I was thrilled.

Cory told me all about his success later that night. "I went back to the restaurant to fill out some new-hire paperwork," he said, "and the guy who hired me asked me why we moved here. I told him it was because my dad died. He asked how, and I told him that Dad died by suicide. He said, 'So did mine. I just had a feeling when you walked through the door.'" Cory paused a moment. "I usually don't tell people about what happened."

Was it possible we were exactly where we were supposed to be, that perhaps we'd been guided to our new home? I started to cry, but they were tears of joy. I was happy for Cory. He had made a valuable connection with his boss, who obviously cared for him and could relate to everything he had been through.

As the weeks wore on, I experienced repeated instances of déjà vu, as if I'd been in that house before and our arrival there had been preplanned. It was the strangest feeling.

———◆———

Not long after we had moved into the new house, I drove with my sisters and sisters-in-law, Ann and Sue, to Montpelier for one of Lily's galleries at Angel Light Books and Gifts. Lily would be channeling, and I hoped Mark would come through somehow and communicate with me.

Angel Light sat on Main Street in a hip part of Montpelier, close to the university in Montpelier campus. Equal parts bookstore and metaphysical shop, Angel Light was more than anything else a spiritual resource center. We entered beneath a bright blue awning and were greeted by the smell of incense burning on the windowsill. Books, art, jewelry, stones, yoga supplies, oils, and candles vied for space on the shelves. But we weren't there to shop. Our big group climbed a flight of old wooden stairs to the second floor, where Lily's gallery was being held in a large carpeted room with lavender-colored walls. The moment we entered, we sensed the energy in the room. Indeed, the lights would flicker more than once that evening.

To my disappointment, Mark didn't come through. But my Aunt Mavis, my mom's sister, did, and she talked to us a little bit . . . and kind of slapped our hands on a few things. Sue's grandfather came through because he had some unfinished business. And Ann's mother, who had died four years earlier, came through. I was grateful my sisters and sisters-in-law had positive experiences.

I was sure Mark didn't come through because he wanted to stay close to me and because Lily would not have approved. Mark was supposed to be in the healing place, not living with me. He was too close to me. I could feel him.

<hr/>

We had built the lake house for our retirement . . . prematurely. We had also built it for Mark's depression. But from the very beginning the house that was supposed to save my husband felt evil as if it had a life of its own. Maybe it was the fact that it had been built on an Indian reservation, or maybe it was more about Mark's depression. I don't know. The house just always felt off. I can't say I ever felt like we belonged there. But I can say that ultimately I came to regret the decision to ever build it.

The more I had to deal with Wade, the more I began to feel like Mark was guiding me. He had never approved of Wade, a slick businessman who had become successful and wealthy by taking advantage of people. I knew Wade was taking advantage of me, but I tried not to care. I wanted to keep it simple. I wanted to make a new life for myself and not have to worry about the expenses of the lake house.

Wade was taking advantage of the fact that I wasn't living at the lake. He didn't have access to the inside of the house. He did however have access to the garage, and he put his lawnmower, oil, and chainsaws in there so he could continue to cut the lawn and work on clearing the front woods. He continued to let his kids use the property for recreation, and when I called him on this and tried to talk to him about it, he said he didn't think I would mind.

"Well, we haven't closed yet," I said. "You said if we didn't close by June, you would help me with my house payment in June and July."

He ignored the request. He knew I was upset, but he wasn't going to do anything about it. I was living in Middleburg and only going up to the lake to check on the property, which I didn't do often. When our contract was due to expire the next day, I texted him and reminded him that we were supposed to close. He texted back that he was just waiting to close on his Florida property, after which time he could close on my property. I told him that it would be beyond the date on the contract and that I worried that it might be a problem. He told me not to worry about it.

I left it at that, figuring I had made a commitment and would see it through to the end. But it didn't feel right. Dealing with him was like dealing with a snake, and I knew Mark would have hated it.

CHAPTER 18

ade set up a new closing date for a week after the original closing date of July 15, although there was no new contract drawn up with a specific date. He put me in contact with his title guy, who would do all the work and handle the closing. In the meantime I had just returned from a weekend of volunteering for a triathlon in northern Vermont, where I had been trying to do something other than think about my life and the lake house, when my cell rang in the grocery store. It was Sunday, and I was supposed to close on the lake house the following day. I didn't recognize the number, but I answered anyway.

It was Chloe, a neighbor lady whose cottage sat right next door to the lake house. A stout woman with dark, curly shoulder-length hair, bright blue-green eyes, and a face full of freckles, she worked in the mortgage business. She had a big welcoming smile and a loud, boisterous voice. You could hear her a mile away. She was also very forward and wouldn't hesitate to tell you what she thought or ask you anything. She had no filter. Chloe only used her lake cottage on weekends. I didn't socialize with her much when she was on the lake, but Cory occasionally hung out with Rocky, her son.

"What's going on with your house?" she asked. "There are all kinds of rumors going around that it sold or that it fell through. I figured I'd just call you and ask."

"It's not sold," I answered. "But yes, Wade is buying it."

"How come he's been up there cutting the woods and the grass and everything?"

"I'm sorry about that, but we're supposed to close tomorrow."

"Why hasn't it closed up till now?"

"Well, technically he's out of contract," I said.

"Excuse me?" she asked in disbelief. As someone in the real estate business, she knew Wade had broken a cardinal rule.

"Yes, I understand what you're saying, but we're going to close tomorrow anyway."

"How would you feel about letting my realtor friend show your house?" she asked.

"What?" I snapped tensely.

"Just do me a favor," she said. "Push him back twenty-four hours on the closing. Just tell him you're unavailable, and you have to push it back. That's all I'm asking you to do so my realtor friend can take someone through it tomorrow morning."

I was nervous about changing anything. The last thing I wanted to do was get into trouble with the realtor who had listed the house originally.

"Okay," I said anxiously. "I'm not up there, but my son is. He has a key, so he could meet up with you and give you the key . . . or wait at the house for your realtor friend. Then you'll have to figure out how to get the key back to me."

We eventually arranged to have her realtor friend meet Cory at the house, but the realtor never showed. Tired of waiting, Cory got upset and headed for home.

Chloe then called, wondering where he was.

"He couldn't wait any longer. He had to go home."

"Okay," she said. "Why doesn't he drop off the key in Appleton? I'll pick it up and somehow get it back to the realtor."

I was starting to get nervous. "I'm just not okay with this," I said.

I had another idea.

I called Cory and asked him to go back to the lake house and leave the inside service door unlocked and the alarm off so that the realtor could give her client a tour of the place. But once he had accomplished that, I called Chloe and told her to forget about it. I wasn't comfortable changing my plans so near to the closing date. I was going to close the next day.

When I went to bed that night, I felt a sense of foreboding and started thinking more about it. The next morning I called Paul, the title guy, and told him I was supposed to go to closing. I then asked him if I could push the closing date back twenty-four hours to Tuesday because I had some other things going on and couldn't meet him.

"Can we talk confidentially?" I asked.

"Sure."

I told him what was going on—that we were out of contract, which he was not aware of, that my property had been used for recreation, that Wade had cut the woods down, and that he was supposed to compensate me for my June and July house payments but hadn't done so. I then told him that I was upset about what had happened and that I had an opportunity to show my house to a potential buyer.

Paul recommended that we draw up a new contract and make Wade's offer to purchase contingent on me being reimbursed for the July house payment and for his use of my property. I thought that seemed fair. Paul told me he would present the new conditions to Wade. I agreed and pushed the closing off for twenty-four hours.

By now I was a nervous wreck. I didn't want to sell the house to Wade, but I didn't know if I had the gumption to cross him and seek out another buyer. Everything seemed awfully complicated, and I didn't want to get into trouble. Even in the best of circumstances, selling the lake house would have been difficult. But Wade, preying on my vulnerability, had drawn out the process, turning what should have been a relatively easy transaction into a three-month odyssey. I felt abused. I had continued to pay the mortgage on the lake house while he had defaced the property and recreated on it. I was sobbing by the time I spoke with Chloe.

"I don't know if I can make it happen," I said.

Chloe wouldn't let me off the hook. "Put your big girl pants on and do this, honey. You can do this!"

"Okay," I said anxiously.

I hung up and called Jay, an attorney Ann had recommended to me. I needed to find out what my rights were.

"Have you cashed the earnest money check?" he asked.

"No," I said. "It's sitting right here. I never cashed it."

"Good, because that's the only way you can eliminate him as a buyer altogether. He's out of contract. You didn't cash the earnest money check. So what you would have to do is send him a release stating that you are returning the earnest money and he is no longer able to purchase the property."

"Okay," I said, feeling relieved.

"Do you want me to send you a copy of that document?" he asked.

"Sure," I said, "send me a copy."

I called Molly, the realtor I had originally listed the house with, a friend of a coworker. She was short and stout, and she had short black hair. In her fifties she was quite pretty and was always dressed in hip clothes. Since I'd canceled my contract with her when Wade had asked for an exclusion to purchase the house, I needed to make certain that everything was legal on that end.

"No, we're not in contract anymore," she said. "I'm really sorry if he doesn't buy the house, but we would have to start all over and have a new contract drawn up."

"That's fine," I said.

I was okay with Molly and knew what I had to do legally to eliminate Wade as a buyer. In the meantime I had told Chloe that her realtor friend, Sandy, could take this couple through my house. The couple loved it immediately; it was everything they were looking for. I was willing to sell it, but we had to keep the original closing date, which was the following day, and it had to be a cash buy. There couldn't be any sort of inspection of the home or the well either. The buyers would have to sign a waiver to all of that because that was the kind of deal I'd signed with Wade.

The realtor called me back. "They loved it, and they want to buy it," she said. "They will adhere to all conditions."

"Oh, my God," I said.

I called Paul, the title guy. Before I said anything about what had just transpired, I wanted to find out what Wade's reaction to the new contract had been. I listened quietly as Paul gave me the bad news.

"He wouldn't agree to the deal," Paul said.

In fact, Wade had told him he wouldn't give me a dime. He was going to buy the house, but on his terms. If I didn't like it, he would pick up his toys and march down the lake with them and put them on his other property.

That was all it took to send me into a rage. He had put his stuff on my beach without asking, had cut down my front woods, and hadn't honored our original deal. I was furious.

"No deal," I said. "Tell him that the deal's off and that he'll get the earnest money and the new document stating that we no longer have an agreement in the mail."

I needed to have that document in the mail before we could close with the couple, so the following morning we set up a closing. Paul agreed to close the new deal even though he was best friends with Wade. He didn't like the way Wade had taken advantage of me.

As nervous as I was, I found comfort and strength in the fact that I was doing the right thing. The couple buying the house had grown children and grandkids. There would be a family in the house instead of a slick, unethical businessman. It felt like it was what Mark would have wanted.

Eva, Cory, and I packed a bag, got up Tuesday morning, and headed for the lake, with Eva's boyfriend joining us for the trip as well. We let ourselves into the cottage, which was just a quarter of a mile from the lake house. I couldn't get myself to go to the lake house yet. I had too much anxiety. Cory went down to the lake house and started getting the boat ready so we could take it to Burlington. The boat was originally supposed to be sold with the house. It was Mark's baby. He had loved it and would not have wanted Wade to have it. I really didn't want to drag it down to Montpelier and throw it in the garage. I didn't need any more responsibilities. But it was ours, and we had to remove it.

Cory hooked up the boat to his truck and headed to Burlington to have it repaired. In the meantime I was waiting at the cottage when my cell phone rang. I didn't recognize the number, but I picked up.

It was the realtor.

"We have a problem," she said.

My stomach sunk, and I began to shake.

"Paul is parked by the side of the road. He got a call from Wade's attorney, who said that if this sale goes through, shit's going to hit the fan, and we're going to be sued."

"You're kidding me," I said.

"Paul is waiting for his boss to give him the green light. I told my boss, who's doing some research."

I assured the realtor I had put the new document and the earnest money in the mail, which meant there was no contract. I had done everything legally that I needed to do.

"I'm going to take this information back and make sure everyone is aware of that," the realtor said.

We got off the phone, and my phone rang again about fifteen minutes later. I figured it was her, so I didn't look at the number. But it wasn't her. It was Wade's attorney.

"If you go through with this sale," he warned me, "shit's going to hit the fan."

"Excuse me?" I said.

"You cannot sell that property. You're still under contract with Wade."

"I'm not under contract anymore," I said. "This is what's going on: He didn't close by the date on the contract. I never cashed his earnest money. I sent him the document stating that he was no longer a buyer on this property, releasing me and him from any legal commitment. I turned the other way when he put all his toys on my beach, utilized my property for recreating, and cut my front woods down. He refused to compensate me, and he refused to sign a new purchase agreement with stipulations that he reimburse me for the July house payment and for occupancy, which he originally agreed to do. He's lucky I don't sue *him*, but I'll turn the other way if this sale goes through today. Otherwise, we will have a legal battle."

"Let me get this right," the attorney said. "He's been occupying your property, and he destroyed part of the property?"

"That's correct," I said.

"Okay," he said. "That's all I need to know."

He hung up, and my daughter and her boyfriend emerged from the kitchen, where they had been standing during our conversation.

"Wow, Mom," Eva said, "you really stood your ground. We're so proud of you. I really didn't think you had it in you."

Within an hour and a half I was standing in my kitchen, closing the deal with the new buyers. It felt awful to be selling the house we had built to save Mark, but I also knew this was the best-case scenario. We were selling it for more money than Wade had agreed to pay, and it was a clean deal, a *cash* deal. For my part I didn't have to do anything else. I was already moved out of the house and could just pick up the check and walk away. I knew right then that Mark had guided us and made it happen. Despite all the resistance I had persevered. I could have backed out, but something had kept me going. Somehow it had all come together at the last minute.

It was July 21, 2009. One year, three months, and eight days had passed since Mark's death, and I'd finally found my big girl pants, as Chloe called them. I was going to be okay. Some of my skills had returned—not all of them certainly—but something had happened that day. I had found a piece of me. Part of Kandace was back. And I knew Mark was right by my side.

CHAPTER 19

After we wrapped up the sale, I decided to stay with the kids at the cottage for a few days. I wanted to make sure that Wade wasn't going to pull anything. It was obvious he had tried to take advantage of me during a vulnerable time in my life, and there was no telling how he would react to losing the deal. He had already sneaked up to the house and retrieved the things he'd put in the garage to hide any evidence he'd been there. But he still hadn't taken any of his things off the shoreline. We gave him a few days to have them removed. Otherwise, they would become the property of the new owners. He did eventually remove them but not before he sent me nasty text messages in an attempt to belittle me.

After we stayed up there for a few days, we went *home* to Middleburg. The boat had been fixed, so we picked it up on our way home to start the next chapter of our lives. We arrived home, unlocked the house, entered through the kitchen, and found a blue comb sitting on the counter. My husband had worn a goatee and had always kept his combs all over the place—in his car, in his shaving kit, in his snowmobile. Blue, red, or purple, they were cheap combs, the kind you would buy in a variety pack.

My daughter had walked in first, and when she saw the comb, she said, "That's not funny."

"What do you mean?" I asked.

"Well, look at this comb," she said.

"Where did it come from?" I asked.

"I don't know," Eva said. "But it's not funny."

Cory, who was outside backing the boat into the garage, yelled for us. "Mom, Eva!" he called. "Come out here!"

We ran outside.

"I was taking the cover off the boat," he said excitedly, "and from underneath, a golf ball rolled out."

The golf ball had Spirit Minerals company logo on it. While he was working there, Mark had made some of his closest friends and had been his healthiest.

"Where did this come from?" I asked. "I haven't seen those balls in forever."

Mark's golf bag wasn't even in the garage. It was in the basement in storage.

"I don't know," Cory said. "It just came rolling out from underneath."

First the blue comb . . . and then the golf ball. Their mysterious back-to-back appearance was simultaneously eerie and comforting. I knew Mark was with us. He was overjoyed we had brought the boat home and hadn't sold the house to Wade. Finally after months of stress and indecision, I was looking forward to settling into my new life. I liked our new home. I was close to my mom now. The kids had jobs. But not long after we found the items, things started to feel off again, and our bad dreams returned.

One night in late July, the weather was so hot that I opened the sliding glass door off my bedroom, making sure to keep the screen door closed and locked. The light breeze felt wonderful, but as I basked in the fresh air, I thought of Mark, who had always been concerned about our safety and had always made sure everything was locked up tightly—almost too tightly sometimes. But that was the way he was. I started to doze off, but the thought that I should lock up nagged at me.

I opened my eyes and saw Mark standing in the screen doorway, right arm outstretched, right index finger pointing at me. Startled half to death, I curled into a ball, pulling my knees up to my chest. My heart pounded as I stared at him. And then *poof*—he was gone. *This cannot be happening again*, I thought. His appearance wasn't comforting; it was frightening. It took me forever to fall asleep, but when I did, I dreamed I was in this crowded place, maybe a bar, and he was there. I was trying to get his attention. I was trying to walk by him, and it was as if he didn't even know me.

From that night on my dreams grew more disturbing and disconnected. He was with us, but he didn't know he was dead. Once again he was trying to be a part of our lives. I felt like I was living with a ghost again, and all the work I had done to help Mark move to a better place, the healing place, had failed. I was at a loss as to how I was going to help him again.

Then as July drew to a close, I received a friend request on Facebook from Jack, my old flame from college, the man I had dated just before Mark. Jack wanted to know how I was doing. I jotted back a note saying that it had been a tough year but I was doing all right. I then brought him up to speed on various details in my life, including the move to Middleburg. After I pushed the *send* button, a chat box window opened up on my computer.

Oh, my God, Jack instant-messaged me. *Is that really you?*

Yes, I replied.

My God. I haven't talked to you in thirty years.

I know.

He asked what had happened with Mark and how I had spent the last three decades. And just like that, we began a relationship over the Internet, chatting regularly and slowly getting reacquainted. As we traded e-mails, I learned that while Jack and I had dated in college, Mark had actually asked Jack to back off because *he* wanted to date me.

Mark, I knew, didn't approve of our newly developing relationship, and one night just to prove it, he started messing with our computers. Mine started acting strange, but Jack's totally crashed. He couldn't get online, couldn't get the thing to reboot, couldn't get it to function at all. I eventually sent him a one-word e-mail that read simply, *Boo!*

When Jack finally got his computer back online, I told him I was still living with ghosts. He asked me what I'd done about it, and I replied that I'd hired a ghostbuster. In fact, I couldn't help wondering if Lily had been talking about Jack when she had said someone would come into my life to help heal my heart.

Mark though wasn't about to make room for another man. One night in August, I was sitting in the living room when I saw him pass down the hall to my bedroom.

Like me, Eva had been having bad dreams again and was unable to sleep. She felt frightened. Then one day she and her boyfriend got lost on their way to the zoo. I had given them vague directions, but after forty-five minutes Eva called me to tell me they hadn't found the zoo.

"You're never going to believe where we ended up," she said.

"Where?" I asked.

"We're at Angel Light."

"Why are you there?" I asked.

"I don't know," Eva said "We got lost, and we ended up on Main Street right in front of Angel Light. There is a woman here who does soul clearing, and I'm going to go in and talk to her. I feel drawn to go in there and talk to her. Her name is Misty."

"Okay," I said.

It seemed we were always led back to Angel Light.

Eva went in for a fifteen-minute reading with Misty, and after her time was up, she called me to recount what she had learned. During the session she had told Misty that Mark was still around and possibly not in a good place. Misty had then confirmed he had crossed over but hadn't gone any further. If he didn't get rid of the bad entities that had attached themselves to him now, Misty had insisted, they would follow him into his next life. He had failed many times in other lifetimes and wanted to get rid of them once and for all.

"You need to come down here and talk to her, Mom," Eva said.

Here we go again, I thought. *Round two.*

I drove downtown to Angel Light and met Misty in a tiny, dimly lit backroom, which was only separated from the rest of the store by a curtain. Misty, an older woman with long, graying hair, sat on the other side of a small table. She was an intuitive who specialized in *soul clearings*. She wore glasses but often removed them while she was speaking to us.

"He's still here," she said of Mark. "He's not a ghost anymore, but he didn't go any farther. He crossed over and stayed on the first astral plane. He needs help to get rid of the attachments and to move on."

When Mark had originally crossed over, we had cleared our spaces. But it was apparent that Mark hadn't been cleared. He was still suffering with the bad entities that had helped cause his death. I arranged to have Misty do a soul clearing for myself, Eva, and Mark. This would clear us of any bad entities, give us psychic protection, and allow Mark to move to a better place, a place from which he could visit us in a more helpful way.

Amazingly after Misty finished the soul clearing, we started having more positive things happen in our lives. Even Cory enjoyed a turnaround of sorts. Through Misty's soul clearings, Eva and I learned a lot about ourselves and our gifts, why we were able to communicate with Mark through our dreams, and why we were able to see him and know he was around. I was blown away by Misty's assertion that in other lifetimes, my daughter and I had had training in helping souls cross over.

Eva was clearly quite gifted as a psychic. But she had no interest in doing any training to become a medium.

"I have to close my psychic door, Mom," she told me one day. "It's too scary for me."

I was beginning to understand now why she'd had night terrors as a child and had always been afraid at night. She hadn't understood what she was seeing. It didn't surprise me that Mark had been able to pound on those doors and get our attention. Had he not been able to, I'm not sure any of us would still be here. In any case Mark was going to make sure we were all safe. He had work to do. We didn't know this yet, but so did we.

CHAPTER 20

After the soul clearing with Misty the problems with Jack's computer disappeared. I began to feel better, more relaxed, happier.

As fall settled in, I learned Lily was going to be at a gallery in Montpelier on Friday, October 13, which was my birthday, so I made reservations for Eva and me. Eva was excited to see Lily, but when I invited Cory along, he made it clear he wanted nothing to do with her or anything medium-related. He was still too wrapped up in his own grief and anger and wasn't ready to forgive his dad or communicate with him. I felt bad and thought he probably could make some peace if he saw Lily.

In the meantime Jack was going to be in the area for a couple of family functions, so I told him I had tickets to the college football's homecoming game in October.

"Really?" he asked.

"Yes," I replied, "and if you're in the area and you can make it work, you might as well come to the game."

He ended up flying in on a Thursday, and I picked him up at the airport and took him back to the house in Middleburg, where he spent the night. Jack still had a strong, athletic body and those amazing, electric blue eyes, although his dark hair had begun to gray. I was astonished to find that the connection we had shared thirty years earlier was still there. All those feelings we'd had so long ago still burned brightly. We hung out in the city the next day and took in some sights, chatting and continuing to catch up. For the first time since Mark had died, I felt alive and could remember the person I'd once been. Could there be life after Mark's suicide? That night Jack had to go meet up with some old college friends, but he returned a few hours later and spent the night once again. When Saturday finally rolled around, we went to the football game, and after he attended a postgame family function, he returned to Middleburg for the night. He was supposed to fly out on Sunday, but he ended up missing his flight and spending one last night with me. He finally went home on Monday.

After he left, I was still reveling in the warm glow of his visit. He was a healthy, happy man, and spending the weekend with him had given me something I hadn't had in years—hope for the future. Eva and Cory, on the other hand, were furious. Clearly suspicious of this new man in my life, Cory had been polite but wary while he had first met Jack. But when it had become clear that Jack and I shared a romantic connection, Cory had left for the weekend and hadn't returned until Jack was on a plane back home. Eva had spent the weekend at school but had heard all about Jack. If Jack's visit had filled me with optimism, it had left her and Cory feeling threatened.

"You're a widow," Eva told me angrily, "and you should behave like a widow."

As desperate as I was to break free of my painful past, my kids appeared to want me to remain steeped in it forever. Hurt and angry, I once again found myself in the destructive but familiar pattern of trying to make everybody else happy. What about me? Did I have a right to happiness?

My relationship with Jack had needed little to ignite again—just a bit of oxygen. Despite my kids' angry reaction to his visit, I was in the best place I had been in a long time. A few days later I drove to Cory's high school to watch my great-nephew play football. He was only in the eighth grade, but his team would be playing on the high school's varsity football field.

Cory was playing volleyball in the high school gym with some of his hockey friends, and after the game Lizzy, Kevin, and I dropped by the gym to watch them play volleyball for a few minutes. The sight of Cory laughing and having fun with his buddies made my heart sing. He'd been miserable for so long.

After we watched a while, Lizzy and I left for a nearby pub to grab a beer. The waitress had just put a beer in front of me when my cell phone rang. I picked up to hear Cory crying hysterically.

"I blew my knee out!" he cried. "I blew my knee out!"

Not again, I thought. "What happened?" I asked.

"I went up to block a spike, and I came down. And my leg got tangled with the spiker's under the net. My other ACL is gone. I can feel it. It's gone."

I was in shock. I picked up my purse, turned to my sister, and said, "I have to go."

I didn't give Lizzy a chance to respond before I bolted out the door. I knew Cory would not be in a good place. Like his dad, he didn't deal well when bad things happened. I worried about him hurting himself all the time like his father had, and to this day I still worry about him, even though he's doing better.

When I got home, I found Cory alone and collapsed on the garage floor, his face in his hands. He was sobbing. It was his left knee this time, which meant he'd been able to drive himself home after the game. But after he had gotten that far, he had crumpled in a heap on the cement floor.

"I can't go through this again," he said through the tears. "I just can't. What am I going to do? I'm not strong enough to go through this again. Why do bad things always happen to me?"

I sat down on the floor with him, not knowing what to do or say. I felt like I was also on the verge of collapsing. I wasn't sure either one of us would survive another surgery . . . or the depression that would surely set in afterward. Then there was the abuse he would surely hurl at me.

"We'll get through this," I said, putting my arms around him. "We don't even know the extent of the damage yet."

"Now I can't go into the military," he cried. "Now I can't go into the military."

I tried to console him, but it was no use. Since Mark's death Cory had been desperate to be part of a family unit, and he had come to think that he might find that sense of belonging in the military. College, he had already decided, wasn't right for him. He had a hard time focusing on anything and was certain he would party all the time and never go to class. I wasn't so convinced that the military was the answer; however, I had been supportive, and at the very least I'd wanted to help him figure out what options were available to him. I had a hunch he was right about college, that he wasn't college material. He was a good student but didn't enjoy school. Most of his fellow seniors were just now beginning to apply to colleges, but Cory had already set his eyes on the military. And now his plans were crumbling.

While I projected a stoic calm, I was reeling inside. *I can't do this*, I thought. *I can't do this.* All I could think about was how much Mark's death had stolen Cory's spirit.

I took him to see a doctor the next day. After the doctor examined his left knee, he referred us to an orthopedic surgeon. Sure enough, the surgeon told us the injury was the same as the one to his right knee. Sometimes such types of injuries were caused by anatomy, but no one ever told us that was the case with Cory.

While Cory was lying low and waiting for his surgery date, he decided he might as well apply to some colleges. What were his options now? He would still research the military as a possibility, but he knew his chances were slim. So he asked Eva for some help with the application process, including the essay. After he mulled over the possibilities, he narrowed his choice to colleges in the New England area, including the university his father had attended, to which he felt more than a passing connection. Mark, Eva, my brother Kevin, my nephew and his wife, and I had all gone there or were now attending that school. Cory saw a sliver of hope, although he didn't really like school and didn't think he was smart enough to make it in college.

CHAPTER 21

A few weeks after Jack's October visit Eva and I were still not getting along. It looked like I would be going alone to the Lily gallery on October 13, or I would go with my brother Kevin, who had generously volunteered to go in Eva's place. But on Thursday, the night before the gallery, Eva called with bad news. She'd just had a huge fight with her boyfriend, Ian, and it appeared they were on the verge of a breakup. Distraught and needing someone to talk to, she set aside her anger toward me and came home the next day just in time for the gallery.

After we grabbed a bite to eat at a local Mexican restaurant, we drove downtown to Angel Light. We then hurried upstairs, eager to see if Lily would be able to channel Mark once again and help us communicate with him. I had a hunch he would make an appearance since it was my birthday.

"Sometimes the messages that come through are for someone in the room," Lily said, addressing the group that had assembled for the reading. "Sometimes they're for someone else, and someone here may be the messenger. Today's message is about suicide, that there's this concept about suicide. When someone commits suicide, they void the contract that they had here. I promise you it gets better. Usually by the age of eight the soul will decide what it needs to master."

I glanced at Eva and could tell she was listening just as closely as I was to what Lily was saying.

"What happens when the soul crosses over after suicide is that they find themselves in the gray space," Lily continued. "The soul is looking for peace or release. Some people commit suicide by choice, and some are influenced. And by that I mean with the help of entities. The soul is able to watch their loved ones while they are in the gray space. People who commit suicide are not bad souls. They are loving souls. In the gray space the soul is able to talk about why they did it, and they are able to watch their loved ones and see what it did to them. There is a divine space where they can go from there—the healing place—but they have to want to go there."

Eva and I traded knowing glances. We knew exactly what Lily was talking about. I wondered if anyone else in the audience did too.

"I want to honor those who have committed suicide," Lily said. "I will go in and help those cross over, those who are stuck. Once they cross over, there is a healing. It may take many lifetimes, but there will be a healing. There is a reason why this group is here at this time together. Tonight we're going to explore the other side to see if there is some message for you."

Lily cleared the space and raised the psychic energy by ringing the Tibetan bell, which centered her and helped increase the vibrations in the room. She then began repeating the names—or rough approximations thereof—of the people who were coming through. Dad or Tadd was likely Mark (still Dad to his kids). Tom or Will was probably Mark's brother, Tom. Lily also saw images of a girl in a Speedo, a girl having to face challenges. Was she me? I swam in a Speedo and had been training for the masters' swim club when Mark died. Lily then acknowledged two more names: Gabby and Ian. Gabby was Eva's best friend and college roommate. Ian was Eva's boyfriend (now husband). It appeared Mark was monopolizing the gallery.

Eva and I were called up to the front of the room, and Lily rang the bell for clarification. Were we the ones the person she was channeling was trying to reach?

She began speaking in a stream of consciousness manner. "Recognize the snow globes—Christmas ornaments—Make sure to be playful with your emotions—Want to see her smile, laugh—Enjoys seeing me happy."

After she explained that she hadn't seen who was talking yet, she mentioned a memory. "Spaghetti dropping—What does it mean?"

I remembered a dish of spaghetti that Cory had dropped while we were camping one time. It had been our only food that night, but we'd all laughed at the mishap.

Mark was using the memory to get my attention.

"I see him now," Lily said. "He's laughing."

My mind was racing. As I thought about the Christmas ornaments, I felt a surge of emotions.

"He wants us to know he is happy he can communicate with us," Lily continued. "He's saying the kids really treasure the ornaments."

She addressed me directly. "Did you almost pass out during the funeral? When you were feeling that feeling, he was hugging you. It was too overwhelming for your energy field. He says he just wants to hold us all again, and he wants to be the one to comfort us and tell us everything is going to be okay. But it hasn't been okay since he crossed over."

Eva and I began to cry.

"Because of the depth of love you feel for him, when love comes into your life, we will always have a higher standard. Don't choose less for yourself." Lily leveled her gaze at Eva and me. "Don't waste time and energy on things that don't matter."

We both knew she was speaking Mark's words. It was almost like he was speaking directly to us.

"I wish I would have just stopped, held your hand. It would have made a big difference." Lily looked at us. "You had the dream, but

139

the dream we strove for financially is not the dream he values most now. And you guys had some wild fights, and most of the time you were right. He said that to see you laugh. Do you put his ring on and off?"

"Yes," I answered. "I wear it around my neck and slide it on and off all the time."

"He loves it when you do that."

"Wow!"

"There's something he would like you to do as a family. He would like you all to go on a vacation by the ocean or the beach and talk about him. He loves that. It gives him a big head. He wants me to tell you if you were in a room of drop-dead gorgeous women, he would only look at you. And when you meet in another lifetime, it will be the same. He will be drawn to only you. He wants to tell you that, even though it was less frequent in the end behind closed doors. If he had to do it again, he would take his time—and don't come a-knockin' if the room's a-rockin'. And then he laughed. He's telling me how scared he was when the children came and those kids raised me. Anything I tried to slip by authority in my day they were better at, and it shows their intelligence."

Lily turned to Eva and began to speak to her. "When you need him, imagine him holding you. Created by love, honey—you could have that stamped on you. Sometimes you're going to be having difficulty making decisions 'cause you want to stay close to home, but you have many things to experience away from home. Please have trust and faith in your mom. She isn't going anywhere soon. There will be little souls coming into this family. He is fun. It's almost like he has this can-do attitude—The best parts of our family were when we didn't have a plan—He has his money on you. He believes in you—You haven't stopped thinking about him, and sometimes you don't want to listen to him. And that's how you build character. But he knows you don't always listen. He knows you are sad, but it's the sadness that helps you remember. Please listen to him sometimes. He does have things to tell you that are important."

After the gallery reading Eva and I walked down Main Street, arm in arm. We were both giddy and laughing and felt close again. We ended up walking into a nice pub, where we sat down and took out our notes from the gallery. As we relived the experience, our conversation focused on Mark, where he was, and how his personality hadn't changed at all. He was exactly the same as he had always been. It was almost like we had just spent time with him. We felt a sense of peace and contentment, but at the same time I missed him greatly and was filled with an overwhelming sadness in knowing that he wasn't coming back.

I found comfort in the fact that Mark was still there to guide me. He had chosen Lily as his medium and obviously trusted her enough to speak through her. She had helped him leave the gray space and cross over into the light, and now she was helping Eva and I heal as well. To this day I believe she helped save my life.

As November drew to a close, Cory was surprised to receive acceptance letters from three colleges. Unfortunately UVM, his first choice, had put him on a waiting list, which meant his future was still uncertain. He was crushed. Nothing, it seemed, was going his way. With no choice but to wait, he grew more anxious and depressed by the day. He was fighting to stay afloat.

His surgery was scheduled for December 18, which was right before Christmas break, so he wouldn't have to miss much school. He wasn't involved in any kind of sport, and he could still walk as long as he was careful and wore a small brace on his knee. Surgery therefore wasn't urgent, at least according to his surgeon. Nevertheless, the wait seemed to go on forever.

I told him I thought he would become too anxious if he stayed home from school, so he continued to go. But he couldn't play volleyball with his friends. He couldn't shoot baskets. He couldn't do anything that he wanted to do. He had just begun hanging out with a group of active boys, but when the whole dynamic of his friendship with them collapsed, he became a couch potato. He would lie on the couch and belittle me, throwing insults at me one after the other. In reaction to the abuse I began to feel helpless and depressed. I was certain I couldn't be beaten down any farther. But I was wrong.

When Cory finally had the surgery, I drove him to and from the hospital and then helped him pack the knee in ice. For the first few days of his recovery he was anchored to the couch. As had been the case after his first surgery, his body reacted violently to the procedure. He ran a fever for three weeks while blood seeped from the wound. Once again he became depressed and verbally abusive. And once again he got hooked on the pain medication.

"It's just the way you are," the surgeon told him. "You just have to get through it."

Cory took his anger out on me, and it wasn't long before I began to tremble at the slightest raising of his voice. I was sick to my stomach most of the time and couldn't eat. Then one day I realized I didn't want to take it anymore. I started avoiding him and wouldn't even walk into a room if he was there. Cory had always had anger issues, but they had grown far worse after Mark's death. I had often told Mark while he was still alive not to leave me alone to raise him. I had been half-joking at the time. But I wasn't laughing anymore.

Eva came home for the holidays, and not long afterward we both began having strange and fascinating visions. I dreamed one night that Katherine, my old high school friend who had contacted me on Facebook, was at a Lily gallery with me . . . and was supposed to be there. The dream, which was extraordinarily lifelike, was what I would come to call a "visitation dream." Many of my dreams were jumbled or surreal and usually difficult to remember when I woke up. But visitation dreams were different. They were as real as anything I experienced while I was awake and felt as though they had actually happened.

Meanwhile, Eva had a visitation dream in which a man was hit by a vehicle and was dying on the road. A few nights later she had the first of several visitations. She was visited by a cat, which was sitting on her nightstand, and then the cat would disappear. She also dreamed that her father was trying to tell her something about an accident she'd been seeing in her dreams.

When she told me about her visions and dreams, she was most curious about the man she had witnessed dying on the road. She had actually seen him standing in her room but had no idea who he was. I started putting all the pieces together. Bret, Katherine's husband, had died after he had pulled onto the side of the road and walked into oncoming traffic, although there was still some mystery surrounding the circumstances. Why had he pulled over? Why had he committed suicide and walked into traffic? I also knew from her Facebook posts that Katherine had put her cat down. Was Eva dreaming about Bret? Did the cat in her dreams belong to Katherine?

I e-mailed Katherine and, after I explained that Lily was a gifted medium whom I had seen a few times, I told her that I'd had a dream about her being at a gallery with me. I also asked her what her cat looked like, hoping to identify the cat for Eva. She sent me a picture of her cat, and sure enough, after I described it to Eva, Eva said it was the cat that had been sitting on her nightstand. I wrote back to Katherine and told her about Eva's dreams, telling her I was certain she was supposed to go see Lily with me. I truly believed that I was being guided by either her husband or Mark and that it was important for her to come with me to the gallery so she could see Lily. Somebody was pushing hard.

CHAPTER 22

Katherine was intrigued but skeptical. She said she had thought about seeing a medium but had always tucked the idea away, feeling foolish. I needed to talk to her face-to-face, so I pushed for us to meet. Because we lived about an hour away from each other, we agreed to meet halfway at a pizzeria.

When we met at the restaurant, I felt an immediate sense of calm and happiness, like everything was right with the world. A school nurse, Katherine exuded warmth and kindness. (I've come to see her as the kindest woman I know.) She stood a heavyset five feet four inches tall and had the same pretty face I'd known in high school. Her blue-green eyes hinted at the heartbreak she'd endured since losing Bret, her soul mate and high school sweetheart. The two had made a striking pair, with Bret towering over Katherine by more than a foot. Bret had been a physical education teacher and basketball coach, and though his height had intimidated some, his big, gentle brown eyes had told a different story. I've often felt that they fell in love while so young precisely because his journey was going to end sooner than hers.

Our meeting also felt guided by divine forces. We had been brought together for a reason. We hugged and then sat down and began to share our experiences. As we discussed our grief and the way it had affected us, I found solace in knowing I wasn't the only person who'd been driven to near insanity by my loss. I learned more about the mystery surrounding Bret's apparent suicide and then shared everything I knew about Eva's visitation dreams, what Bret had shown her.

"I'm not sure about the whole medium thing," Katherine said. "I've thought about it many times, but I'm not sure."

"Just think about it," I said. "I'll let you know when Lily's going to be back here again."

With the holidays upon us I knew Lily wouldn't be in the area again until January, so I told Katherine I would keep her informed of the medium's next appearance in Montpelier and left it at that. The rest of our meal was spent catching up, and from that day on the little pizza joint became one of our regular meeting places. In the weeks and months ahead we would spend numerous long lunches there, staying through shift changes and earning a reputation as the two ladies who talked far more than they ate or drank, although we always enjoyed a few glasses of wine with our meals.

A few days later I e-mailed the dates of Lily's next visit to Montpelier.

Okay, Katherine replied, *I'm in.*

From there I took charge, made the reservation, and sent Katherine my address so she could meet me at my house early on a Saturday morning and travel downtown to Angel Light for the gallery.

Not surprisingly Katherine was nervous about going to see Lily. Her two children didn't believe in mediums, although they did want to see her get healthy and move forward. It had been a little over a year and a half since we'd lost our husbands, and I think I was probably doing better than she was. I had made peace with Mark's death, but she still had several unanswered questions about Bret's.

The coroner and police officials had stated that her husband had died by suicide. According to the official report, he had deliberately pulled over to the side of the road and walked out into traffic. But in her heart she had never bought the story. There had been no note. They had just enjoyed a wonderful family vacation. Nothing had pointed to suicide. As a result she had never accepted his death. Meanwhile, she had fought with the school district where he'd taught to host some kind of memorial basketball tournament in his honor, but the school had refused because of the nature of his death. I knew the feeling. I had approached an organization concerning a memorial for Mark, but they never called me back. Death was the same, of course, whether a person died by suicide or from an illness. But suicide carried with it an undeniable stigma.

When the day of the gallery arrived, I was just as nervous as Katherine was when she arrived at my house. I knew I had been guided by some external force to take her to see Lily, but what if she had a bad experience at the gallery? I was praying she would get some answers.

As usual, my husband was the first one to come through at the gallery. He was pushy when it came to Lily. He probably thought she belonged to him, I thought jokingly. He was able to tell me some things he hadn't told me before, but one message he relayed to me resonated on a spiritual level: "There isn't anything we do," he said, "that God won't forgive us for." That left me with the most profound sense of peace and understanding I had ever experienced. I knew Mark was having a tough time forgiving himself, but God had already forgiven him.

I've since come to believe it will take him a long time because it's not like you die and are instantly happy. You take all your baggage with you, not just the love, and you have a lot of healing to do, depending on how you lived your life. Thus, it makes sense to live your life here in a good and honest way. Love people and treat them the way they should be treated, the way *you* want to be treated, with respect and kindness but most of all with love. Pay close attention to your actions and to the decisions you make.

After Mark finished speaking through Lily, I began to worry about Katherine's husband. Would he come through? Bret had been shy and not pushy while he had been alive. It stood to reason that he would be shy on the other side too. But he finally came through toward the end of the gallery, standing quietly behind Katherine. I could feel him. A distraught Katherine was sobbing so hard she couldn't speak. Her father was also with Bret. Lily kept saying that her head hurt, and there was no mention of suicide. Every time my husband would come through, she would say, "This man took his own life." But when Bret came through, all she kept saying was that her head hurt.

"Something happened in his head," Lily repeated. "Something happened in his head."

Katherine was so upset. I tried to answer questions for her. Lily said she needed to be loved, hugged, and supported and that she needed to let people help her. She then channeled Bret.

Bret had not died by suicide, we learned. It had not been his choice. He had suffered a brain aneurysm while he had been driving to the hospital. Aware that he was in trouble, he had made the conscious decision to pull over so he wouldn't take any other souls with him. By the time he had stepped out of the car, he was already going to the light. He hadn't felt the car hit him because the aneurysm had already taken his physical body.

"It was his time to go," Lily said.

Katherine had known in her heart that he hadn't taken his own life, which was why she had been unable to accept Bret's death. Now she knew the truth, and I could hear the joy in her sobbing. Her tears of relief still haunt me because they touched my soul so deeply. I was filled with gratitude toward Lily for helping my friend.

After Lily wrapped up the gallery, Katherine and I decompressed over pizza and wine, spending the rest of the day and evening together. Once again we were pretty jazzed. Reconnecting with our husbands had left us feeling healed and energized. I still get chills thinking about Lily's extraordinary healing powers and what she did for Katherine that day. She is an exceptional seer, a gift from God.

Although now on the road to healing, Katherine remained guarded about her experience. She wanted to share it with her kids, who were highly skeptical of mediums, but she didn't know how. How could she convince them that Bret hadn't taken his own life? She decided she wanted to learn more and meet with Lily for a one-on-one session. I happily agreed to take her to the appointment, still several weeks away.

"I might need you to pick up the pieces afterward," she said.

"Absolutely," I said. "I will 100 percent be your person. I believe you're doing the right thing. You should go see Lily. You still have too many questions."

She went in early March, before the two-year anniversary of Bret's death. During the one-on-one session she realized how heroic Bret had been to pull over to the side of the road and avoid endangering any of the drivers around him. He had stepped out of the car because he was dying and didn't know what else to do. Bret talked about his kids and how much he loved them and how he was still there with them, watching over them. He explained that those who crossed over showed up at graduations and other important events and were still very much a part of our lives. That was the part that Katherine and I were struggling with (and still battle to this day). Our husbands were still with us, still seeing everything, but they had departed us physically. Although it was comforting to know Mark was still watching over me, I desperately missed his touch, his voice, his physical presence.

Katherine eventually shared her experiences with her kids, even playing them the CD of her session with Lily. Much to her relief, the moment was cathartic for everyone involved. Her children were glad she had gone to the session and glad it had brought them all together. As I contemplated my role in facilitating their healing, I realized this was part of my journey now and an important part of who I was. I would help people here and on the other side. Help them in the healing process. Help souls who were stuck get to a better place.

CHAPTER 23

*T*hat same month on the two-year anniversary of Bret's death, he came to me in a dream and told me how much he loved the kids. He was young and beautiful and happy. I knew the next day would be tough for Katherine—it always is on the anniversary of a beloved's death—so I reached out to her and told her I had seen Bret the previous night. She had always been pretty amazed by the way my daughter and I could see things in our dreams and connect with the other side.

"Bret is with you and the kids today," I told her. "He's very happy and very much at peace."

"That makes me feel really good today," Katherine said.

Later on in March while she was home on spring break, Eva got a call from one of her old high school friends.

"Do you know Jayne?" he asked.

Jayne, also a former high school classmate of Eva's, was a beautiful, spirited young lady with tall, slim features. She was a junior in college and was on the school's dance team. She was always pushing the envelope, and Eva didn't always approve of her reckless behavior and free-spiritedness.

"Yeah," Eva said.

"They found her dead in Alabama on spring break in her hotel room. She was dead in bed, and nobody knows what happened."

Eva relayed the disturbing news to me, but I said little, not wanting to pry into something so personal. Then Jayne came to me in a dream that night. She was distraught because she didn't know how to cross over and was afraid to leave her family. Mark had struggled with the same quandary and had tried to stay in limbo. Like him at the time, she was in danger of becoming ghostlike rather than a spirit. After Jayne crossed over, she could come back and visit, but she wouldn't be earthbound.

"I don't know where to go," Jayne repeated.

We got down on our knees, and I took her by the shoulders.

"Jayne," I said, "you need to go to the light."

"I can't," she protested. "I can't go there. I can't go to the light."

"You have to go there. You need to go to the light. There are people there who love you and are waiting for you there. Then you can come back and visit."

"Really?" she asked, astonished.

"Yes," I said. "But you need to go to the light first. It will be amazing—more amazing than you could possibly imagine."

"Really?"

"Yes, and then you can come back and visit your family from a much better place anytime you want."

Jayne threw her arms around me and hugged me. "Thank you," she said and went into the light.

When I woke up, I remembered every detail of her face and how she had felt in my arms, the way she smelled of a fresh rain shower. I still remember everything from the dream as clearly as if it had happened yesterday. I've yet to share it with her family because I don't know how they would react. Maybe it would be healing for them, but I don't know. I just don't know. To this day we've never found out what happened to Jayne. In any case the dream convinced me that I had a gift. I was eager to help others however I could.

As the weather warmed, I began to heal. I was hoping to get back to work at a job I loved. I also took a few trips with Jack. He was a good person and a good listener—two qualities that sped up my healing. He understood what I had been through and seemed delighted to witness my slow transformation, which he compared to the tight bud of a rose gradually opening.

"I just can't wait to see you when you're totally open and you take flight," he would say.

Meanwhile, Cory was doing some soul-searching of his own. We talked that summer about his dad's OWIs and how they had led to the perfect storm and his eventual suicide.

We had settled in one evening to watch a movie when he received a text message from a friend.

"He wants to go out," he said.

"Really?" I said warily. "It's kind of late. You know I don't like to be that kind of a mom, but—"

"I know," he said. "But I won't be late."

I got a bad feeling the moment he walked out the door. I had told myself to pay closer attention to those feelings, to trust my gut, which wasn't an easy thing to do, even if I was right 90 percent of the time. I went to bed feeling uneasy and restless.

At 1:30 a.m. my eyes snapped open, and I sat straight up in bed. It was as though someone had shaken me awake. *Okay*, I thought. Just then my cell phone, which was sitting beside me on my nightstand, started vibrating. It was doubtful I would have heard it had I been asleep.

"Hello?" I said after I grabbed it.

It was someone from the Middleburg Police Department. They had picked up my nineteen-year-old son for drunk driving and had him in custody.

I started to shake uncontrollably. My whole world was crashing down around me again. *Oh, my God*, I thought. *Here we go again. How is he going to survive this? How are we going to get past this and be okay? Are we healthy enough to do this?*

I threw on my clothes and went down to the police station to get him. He was still drunk, and although he had cooperated with the police, he was mean to me the moment we got in the car. By the time we pulled into the driveway, he was screaming at me.

"I don't want to live anymore!" he cried. "Dad died because he hated life and didn't want to live anymore! *I* hate life! I hate living without Dad!"

Finally after he kicked a few walls, he went to bed.

Worried that he might take his own life, I called my daughter and alerted her and her boyfriend that I might need them. Then I called Charlie in San Francisco.

"Mom, the weirdest thing just happened as I was lying in bed," he said. "I have this old chandelier in my room, and a lot of the bulbs that have never worked were suddenly going on. They were just clicking on, and I kept wondering, *What's going on?*"

I was certain Mark had woken us up to make sure we were aware of what was happening with Cory. We were all going to need to be there for him. When I had helped Mark cross over with Lily, she had told me that our third child would need extra help. Cory had always needed extra help, so it was no surprise that he would grieve for his father harder and longer than the rest of us. Living without his dad was difficult for him, and it broke my heart every day to see him struggle.

I watched him most of that night to make sure he wasn't going to hurt himself. For my part I couldn't stop shaking. Cory's adventure reminded me too much of the night Mark had gone missing.

Cory woke up feeling awful . . . and angry. He was angry at me most likely because he knew how much he had hurt and disappointed me. We were stuck in a vicious cycle in which all the anger he felt toward his father was directed toward me. I was his valve, and he had plenty to be angry about—the death of his father, two knee surgeries, a move to a new town and school, and now this. How much more could he take? I didn't know how strong we were or how much more we could endure, but I knew we would have to find the strength somewhere.

If his second torn ACL had already dashed his military hopes, the OWI served as a final nail in the coffin. He had no choice but to continue to wait to hear back from UVM, where he'd been wait-listed. Although it was no consolation to him, I was certain he was exactly where he was supposed to be, that the bad things that had happened in his life were guiding him toward his destiny. As Elizabeth Lesser wrote in *Broken Open: How Difficult Times Can Help Us Grow*, sometimes you have to hit rock bottom before you find your way. Cory's challenge was to forgive his father and learn to live without him. Were we at the bottom yet? Sometimes I didn't know if Cory would survive. Would he choose suicide like Mark had? At times I doubted my own survival as well. What kept me going was the determination to be there for my children. Although I was trying to forgive Mark for what he had done, I often struggled with how he could just leave his family.

We drove to Burger Joe's to pick up Cory's truck, which he needed for work. On the way he told me more about the events of the previous night. He had been sitting in his truck in Burger Joe's parking lot, well aware that he was too drunk to drive. But before he could call me or a friend to come and pick him up, someone had notified the police. The simple fact that the keys were still in the ignition had been enough to earn him the OWI. It didn't matter that he wasn't driving and that he was about to call someone for a ride.

When we pulled into the Burger Joe's parking lot, he burst into tears.

"I hate life without my dad. I can't do it. I just can't do it. I can't do this life without my dad. He hated life, and so do I. That's why he left."

"We're going to be okay," I said as tears filled my eyes. "Life does suck without your dad, I know. But we're going to be okay." I was determined to support him. "I love you," I said as he started to get out.

"No, you don't."

"Yes, I do," I insisted.

"How can you love me?" he asked. "How?"

"I'm not mad at you," I answered. "I think you did the right thing by not driving the truck, and I will do whatever I can to help you get through this."

He leaned inside the car and wrapped me in his arms, and we held still for a moment as we each received the love and support we needed. Was everything going to be okay?

CHAPTER 24

ory was allowed to drive until his court date, which was six weeks away. In the interim we learned some good news. He was off the waiting list and had been officially accepted into the University Vermont-Burlington. Unfortunately it was still up in the air whether or not he would get into the dorm.

"I'm not going to get in," he lamented. "I'm not going to get in. What am I going to do? I don't want to go to any other school."

He wanted to be in the woods and enjoy the wide-open countryside, which was what Burlington offered. Unfortunately housing at the school dorm was full at the moment, and if that held up, he'd have to live off campus in a hotel as a freshman until space became available—not an ideal scenario for someone with the uphill struggle he was facing.

"I'm not living in some hotel," he groused. "If I don't get into the dorm, I'm not going to UVM."

I figured he would probably get into the dorm because I had gone to school there and knew that rooms at the dorm almost always opened up at the last minute. But he was focused on the negative, not the positive, which was that he'd gotten into his school of choice.

To his credit he didn't drink after his OWI and spent most of his time at the house, where his friends would come and hang out.

One day Cory was downstairs in the weight room when he thought he saw a pair of eyes looking at him through a crack in the door.

"It scared me," he said after he told me about the incident. "I always feel like there's someone watching me when I'm lifting weights."

He was using his father's weights and his father's weight bench, and Mark's aura was everywhere. But Cory had never really felt that before.

"Do you ever dream about your father?" I asked. It was a question I had put to him before.

"I dream about Dad a lot," he admitted. "We're always recreating, and we're always so happy. Then *poof*—he disappears, and it's like he takes part of me with him. He takes my joy."

When he was younger, Cory had been a funny kid who could do all kinds of impressions that would have us belly laughing. He'd lost that joy after his dad died. Mark and Cory had been so connected that I think part of Cory's soul went with his dad's when he died.

"You need to find a way to get that back," I said, "because the joyful part of you didn't belong to your father. It belonged to you. You have the right to laugh and be happy again."

"I have to tell you something," he said.

"Okay."

"A friend of mine—I can't remember his name because he doesn't hang out here that much—he came over here with a bunch of guys a couple of weeks ago. He pulled me aside and told me he had to tell me something. I asked him what it was, and he said he'd been here a couple of times and every time he was down here he saw something. He said somebody was with me, hanging out with me. He said they appeared like a shadow on the wall, but they were always down here with me. I got really upset and told him to get the hell out of my house. I was that mad. He apologized as he was leaving and told me he'd been able to see things like that since he was a little kid. He said, 'Maybe it's your dad.'"

"You feel like somebody's watching you," I said, "especially when you're downstairs, and this kid saw something that's with you. And then there are your dreams. Cory, I know you've never considered seeing Lily and talking to your dad, but I think you should consider it now after everything you've been through. Maybe it will help."

After he mulled over the possibility, Cory finally agreed to see Lily.

I called Angel Light on a Saturday and asked if there were any one-on-one sessions available with Lily.

"She's totally booked," said the woman who answered the phone.

"Oh, really?"

"Yes," she said. "Let me just check the schedule one more time."

I could hear her turning the pages of the appointment book.

"Oh, my God," she said. "There's a thirty-minute slot here."

"You know," I said, "thirty minutes would be better than nothing."

"No," she said a couple of seconds later. "Somebody made a mistake. There's one forty-five-minute session available on Thursday at 3:30 p.m."

"I'll take it," I said.

When Thursday arrived, Cory woke up in a bad mood. He was agitated and anxious, which was typical of him when it came to anything out of his comfort level, and Lily was definitely out of his comfort level.

"I don't want to go!" he screamed at me.

I started crying. "Do it for yourself," I said, "and me."

"It's stupid," he said. "I'm not doing it." He went up to his room and slammed the door.

Distraught, I called Eva. "He's not going to go," I said between sobs.

"Then you go," she said. "Just go in his place. Maybe it will help you."

I was crestfallen. *How am I going to be able to get Cory to see Lily?* I wondered.

I showered and went about my business that morning, and at about two o'clock in the afternoon Cory came downstairs and said he was going to go.

"Okay," I said.

He was still agitated when we left, and when we ran into road construction on the way, he angrily blamed me for not leaving early enough. I felt like I was going to throw up. Either this was going to help or make things worse between Cory and me. When we hurried into the bookstore, we found out that Lily was running about ten minutes late. This gave us a few minutes to calm our nerves.

After a short wait he went up to meet Lily. But I didn't go with him, and I didn't let her see me either, not that she ever remembered people she had met in one-on-one sessions or at galleries before. (It was a protective mechanism for her. Otherwise, she would have never been able to survive all she saw and heard.)

I walked outside and wandered Main Street before I finally took a seat on a bench across the street from Angel Light. As I nervously watched for Cory to emerge, I kept talking to God and to Mark, praying everything would be all right and that this would be the beginning of Cory's healing. I wanted his session with Lily to be the start of good things for him, but he would have to allow them into his life. As Lynn Grabhorn points out in her book, *Excuse Me, Your Life Is Waiting: The Astonishing Power of Feelings*, you attract what you vibrate, and if you're always in a bad place and always focused on the negative, then bad things will follow you. During the last year I had worked really hard to focus on the positive and look ahead and vibrate at an incredibly high level. I believed good things had come into my life because of that. Now it was Cory's turn to take control of his feelings and his life.

CHAPTER 25

After his forty-five minutes were up, Cory exited beneath the bright blue awning out front of Angel Light's with tears streaming down his face. He was sobbing hard—not an easy thing to do for a nineteen-year-old macho man.

I signaled to him from across the street, and he joined me a moment later.

"Are you okay?" I asked as we walked back to the car.

He nodded yes but said nothing. He was silent during the ride home as well. I figured he needed time to decompress. I knew well what it was like after a session with Lily. He was probably emotionally and physically exhausted.

Not until we reached home and sat down inside was he ready to share a few things from the session, and as I listened to him describe his experience, it became obvious that Lily had saved another member of my family. In the days that followed he remembered more and more details that he wanted to tell me all about. I then had the privilege of listening to the CD Lily had made of their one-on-one session.

After he got his name and address, the first thing Lily did during her session with Cory was help the aura in the room.

"This one's for the heart, which is important," she said, "because I feel a lot of sadness in the room right now. I need you to shuffle the cards as many times as you feel comfortable doing. And when you feel like you've done enough, just tell me. If there's anything you want me to focus on, I want you to tell me what that is, honey."

"My father," Cory said.

"Is he here or on the other side?" Lily asked.

"He's on the other side," Cory said.

"All right," she said. "Now let's see if I can contact him. I want you to pick nine cards from the deck and then put them down one on top of the other."

Cory did as she instructed, and then she counted the cards one through nine.

"I just felt somebody come in," she said. "It's almost like he's been waiting a long time or something. Three cards facedown on top of each other, honey."

She rang the Tibetan bell, and it reverberated in the room as it had done during my sessions with her. Did Cory sense a change in the room's vibration?

"I'm talking to my Aunt Leah," Lily explained. "She's sometimes one of my guides on the other side. She was very helpful to me as a child. She's the one who acknowledged that I had a gift. I asked her if she saw your father, and she said, 'He's right here, honey.' But I don't feel him, and I don't see him either. That's why—I know you're saying that, but I don't see him or feel him—Okay, I feel something coming from this way. I keep seeing this picture. It's a picture of you. It reminds me of outdoors. It's a picture of you smiling, but it's almost like the face is missing. So I'm wondering if the face that's missing is your father's. Was the picture taken outdoors with the two of you doing something? And then it's almost like he's missing—a knowing that he's missing. Then I saw a big ear, which is always a symbol. I always see things in symbols and have to figure out what that means. An ear means, 'I hear you,' or, 'I'm listening to you.' Or it's almost like, 'Listen, you'll hear me.'

"Sometimes you already know what he's going to say without actually having to hear his voice, especially when you're making choices in your life. There's a part of you that can know what he would say or how he would respond, even though you may not feel his presence physically. When I look at you, it's almost like when you watch people play basketball and different types of games. It's almost like I'm watching you. There are things you are doing in honor of him. 'When I do this, I'm doing it in honor of you, or I'm thinking of you.' It's kind of like if I were going to shoot a basket, I would think, *This one's for you*, and then get right in there and shoot the basket. It's like getting in there and feeling that triumphant feeling.

"I do see white in your intuition aura, which means your intuition is very pure. It's not tainted. You're not someone who's trying to make things up. You're not looking at things from a delusional place. That's something I see very clearly. I know you requested your father, but I have to acknowledge everyone I see in your energy field. And one of the things I see is that someone is coming through. To me it looks like something shaped like a kidney in a person's body, and it seems like something's in the kidneys. What I see might be an infection or something not right in the kidneys, like a cancer spreading. So I'm going to acknowledge that. It could be someone other than your father acknowledging that, so I'm just going to say that I acknowledge that.

"I see a dove, which means you have a good sense of humor. Your joy, your laughter, your happiness is just as important to your father now as it was in the past. I need to say that to you. I feel that you're very clear in recognizing the things that are not healthy for you, even though there are some things that you may choose as an escape. It kind of reminds me of when someone does something to excess because they want to comfort themselves so they don't have to feel. I'm being told that there's a part of you that knows that that's temporary and that's something you don't have to invest all your time in. It's a choice that you've made in order to process

161

your feelings, and those feelings also include any grief that you are feeling.

"I feel like this is an opportunity for you to spiritually refuel yourself. You're supposed to be looking for dragonflies. There's a movie called *Dragonfly*, and it would be very symbolic of the relationship you have with your family members. I feel like your father sends you dragonflies, and with you they represent transformation and change. Your soul will go through some major transformation and changes. Although you look quite young to me, sweetheart, I'm going to tell you that your head is very, very mature for your age. It's like you have had some very interesting things happen in your life that have made you kind of grow up. But I have to give you this counsel. I'm going to suggest to you that you'll be an old man soon enough. You have a choice. You can be the old man who is always so serious, or you can be the old man who truly enjoys the adventures and the opportunities that are in his life and who recognizes that death is a part of life. It's part of the cycle of life. It's something that none of us want to experience but all of us will one way or another. Death should be a celebration of your life and the life of the person who has crossed over.

"Even though nothing is really ever perfect, there is perfection in the expressions of love. You will be a great father. All the qualities that you appreciated in your father—you will bring out those qualities. And all the things you didn't appreciate—you will get rid of those things. I'm supposed to tell you that you need to forgive yourself because it feels like you're paying attention now. But so many times we think about the things we should have done. *Why didn't I do this? Why didn't I do that?* Don't do that to yourself. Know that your life honors those who have been a part of your creation in this lifetime. Honor who you are. I see in the center of intuition that you are trying to hold on to things. I see that you have what we call 'the great responsibility.' I feel that you're the person who tries to hold it all together and makes sure it doesn't fall apart. It reminds me of when someone cuts a rope into tiny pieces and then tries to hold everything together. You have to cut yourself some slack sometimes because sometimes that responsibility thing—*I should have done this* or *I should have done that*—harms us.

"There is absolute proof that you are an awesome son. You prove that you are a man by your choices. You have free will, and that enables you to choose a life that is best for you. I wish we could go backward, but I am going to tell you this. You will never forget. You will always bring up those memories. And I want you to hear these words because they are coming from the other side. This is not me. This is a divine voice. 'I am proud of you. Be proud of yourself. I am proud of you. Be proud of yourself.'

"So take a good inventory of yourself, sweetheart, and take a look at how your actions are communicating how you value or devalue yourself. Choose the path that values who you are, and I see in the throat chakra that you could be an excellent negotiator. There is no doubt in my mind that you could even use those negotiating skills to manipulate others, but that is not in your path. I see you as an individual who will be encouraging and supportive. I am going to say this very carefully so you hear it. You will come in contact with young men and boys who have never had a father. You will come into contact with those who can appreciate the nurturing. In other words there will be a time when you will be a coach to others. You will support them. You will encourage them. You will give them that. It's not necessarily the children you bring forth from your loins that are going to benefit from your ability to care, to be nurturing, and to love. It will be like a salute to your father, saying, 'I will not forget.' You are not someone who will drop the ball, okay, sweetheart? You're just not.

"Whenever you have dropped the ball, it was because you just weren't interested. It wasn't worth your time. I'm going to tell you something. When you are ready, you will take responsibility. You will stand, and you will stand your ground. You need to remember that you are not alone, even if it feels like it sometimes, even though you can be very, very afraid. You are not alone. You're not alone—" Lily's voice trailed off.

"He's saying that because I keep hearing it over and over again. I feel that your heart is very receptive to the people you love. You have to watch this with yourself. Sometimes you are going to feel such intense emotion that you may want to punch something or you may want to punch someone or just get it out. My advice would be to get it out in a way that's healthy and not harmful to you or anyone else. You are very good at putting on a tough exterior to protect a soft inside. You are very good at that. I feel like there's a lightning bolt on your heart, which means major transformation and change that shook you up and also shook up the people around you. You realize that you're not the only one who's grieving, and one of the nicest things you can do, one of the coolest things you can do, is sit next to one of those people and just say, 'I'm here. I'm right here.'

"If you trust your heart, you can draw wealth to you. Your emotions actually help you to choose the right path for you. Something is making you pissed off and angry. Unless you are someone who wants to make changes in the law, that is not the right path for you. Okay? You will know that you are going in the right path because the soul will say, 'Yes, this is right.'

"Your father wants to say that he doesn't want you to think that he was ever disappointed in you. He doesn't want you to ever think that." Lily's voice dropped to a whisper. "There he is. He's right behind you. That's why I have my eyes closed—because I can see him better. I can see him when my eyes are open, but I see the energy better when my eyes are closed. There's like this flowing movement, this energy right behind you. His hands are on your shoulders—or someone's, usually a father or grandfather. It's a father figure because they come in right behind. 'Wear it,' he says, 'if it makes you feel better. Wear it.' Maybe *it* was something that was his or something he gave to you or something that was passed on to you. If you wore it, he would be proud, and he would be happy. He would feel good if you would do that. He's not here to freak you out. Don't be afraid.

Don't be afraid. I'm seeing a can of worms being opened, like there's a can of worms around you. I don't know why, but there's some kind of can of worms that is open around you. If I had a can of worms, I'd go fishing. Either that, or put them in my garden because worms represent taking unfertilized ground and making it better. Sometimes the things that seem negative are the things that make things better. He wants to tell you not to quit. Don't quit. You're not a quitter. If you're going to start something, finish it. 'Do it in a way that they know you did it,' he says. Put your style, your signature on life, your way of doing things. Give them something to talk about that inspires."

CHAPTER 26

Cory wept as Lily continued.

"It's almost like when someone is supposed to put the brakes on," she said, "but there's a delay. They don't brake fast enough. There needs to be a brake. That can be symbolic of many things, but I'm going to say stop. Stop something.

"I'm down in the center of passion. You have an ostrich. Ostriches are really fast, and you have to be careful when it comes to your passion. Because when you move too fast without prior planning, it brings piss-poor performance. In other words, be prepared, especially when passion is being called. Be prepared for yourself. I don't know what you've decided for yourself during those moments, but ostriches move too fast. It's like the soul just needs to slow it down every once in a while. Slow it down. Go at your own pace. There's no need to go so fast. Man, you have a lot of tanks around you, like you're on the defensive or something. I don't know why you're on the defensive, but it's like you're prepared for any battle. You have these tanks around your energy field. That could mean that you feel you have to be the fierce protector, the protector of all that is.

"He keeps saying how much he loves you. Do you know? I just heard the word *Henry*. I don't know what that means. But since I had a relative named Henry, I just have to make sure not to put my stuff into your session. That doesn't mean that's your father's name.

It could be somebody that's here or on the other side. It could be symbolic for something else.

"'God, did I ever love you.' Honey, how did your father die?"

"He died by suicide," Cory answered.

"Can you tell me who on the other side had difficulty with their kidneys and their kidneys shut down before they crossed over?"

"I don't know," Cory said. "My cousin had some problems with his kidneys and had a kidney transplant."

"He got a kidney transplant?" Lily asked.

"Yes," Cory said. "He's fifteen."

"It may be an acknowledgment, however the transplant happened. I understand the spreading of the disease. Say your father's first name for me, sweetheart."

"Mark."

"I know," Lily whispered. "It wasn't your fault. You didn't do anything wrong. Can you explain something to me? Why do I keep seeing a car involved? Why am I seeing a car? Tell me about the car."

"He died in a car."

"Okay. Thank you. I feel like his soul—It's almost like—How do I explain it to you? Remember when I told you to put the brakes on? It feels like he wanted to stop, but he didn't stop soon enough. It was almost like, 'What the heck is happening here?' I have to say it the way I see it, honey. He's talking about a vacation, and he's showing me this picture. But he's not in the picture. He might be acknowledging a vacation that you guys went on, or there was a vacation prior to his crossing over. What's with the vacation?"

"We used to go on a lot of vacations," Cory said.

"Outdoors?" Lily asked.

"He and I would go snowmobiling."

"Then you must have either gone. Or you think about it or him, and you want to go. The way he's talking about it—" Lily's voice trailed off. "He was under a lot of pressure. A lot of it he put on himself. That's not an excuse for his choice. It's not an excuse. He's calling you his best friend. He thinks that you were his best friend, as close as anyone could have been to their father. He says you're his best friend, honey."

Cory began to cry harder.

"He says his crossing over was a disappointment for everyone, and actually—I'm going to say it the way I see it—people were really shocked when it happened. They were really shocked. 'Me, too,' he says. Right now he's in a very, very lovely place, a space that reminds me of outdoors, a place that's just very, very free. He's very peaceful. He told me you were always a great son, and he's sorry for any pressure he put on you, and the only expectation that he has of you is for you to be happy. But part of your soul repeats back to me, 'How can I be happy without you, Dad? How can I be happy without my dad by my side? How can I be happy knowing my dad died by suicide?'

"I'm going to say this to you, honey," Lily continued. "There's no doubt in his mind that he was loved. Never for one moment has he doubted that you have loved him. Was there some time of graduation recently? Because I see a cap and gown. Was there a graduation?"

"I just graduated."

"He was right there, honey. Did anyone take digital photos? You have to look at those photos because he'll come in orbs. They look like orbs in the photos. He tried to take a picture right next to you so that you could see him because he was so proud of you. Do you want to talk to him, honey? Do you have anything you want to say to him? 'Please, ask him to talk to me,' he keeps saying. I can try to respond, and I can't make anything up. Right now he keeps saying, 'I love you. I love you. I love you.' He keeps saying it over and over again."

Cory continued to sob. "Just tell him I love him," he said.

"'You tell me every day,' he says."

Cory sobbed harder. "I just don't know what to do without you."

"Okay," Lily said. "I'm going to repeat this exactly the way he's saying it. 'Sooner or later one of us was going to be without the other, and the thought of not being with you was very difficult for me. I can't apologize enough. My choice was selfish. But you know, son, I could have stopped. I could have stopped, but it just got to the point where it had gone too far.' This was not a choice he would have done to himself. You know, honey, I have to say something to you. I don't know anything about your dad, so I'm just going to tell you something I know as a seer. Sometimes when somebody is upset about something in their lives, even if they look okay, sometimes people will take something. They'll take a substance of some sort that's going to help them get through it. Sometimes when people do that, especially if they drink to excess, they create holes in their aura. And when you create holes in your aura, there are cockroaches in the universe that like to destroy families. They love to do that. That's why when people get really drunk they don't remember what they did. And it's like there's this feeling around your father that when his soul realized what was going to happen, he tried to stop it. But it was too late. There is no excuse. Over and over again he says that he has had to learn to forgive himself, and 'I still haven't.'"

Chapter 27

"'Some of the best times in my life were the ones I spent with you,' your father says."

Cory kept sniffling.

"Sometimes your father felt like he didn't meet everyone's expectations. This was a good man. This was a quality man. But sometimes he just felt like he failed and there was nothing more he could do. He says, 'The truth always surfaces—always.' Honey, do you have a sister? I want to acknowledge the sister. I have a message for her. He absolutely loves her. He's counting on you to protect her. She gets messages from him all the time. Somehow she's getting messages from him. You are too. He's acknowledging two significant females, honey."

"My mom and my sister," Cory said.

"Keep going," Lily said to Mark. "I heard you, sir."

She directed her comments back to Cory. "He told me to tell you that your mom is in a better place than she has been in a long, long time. It's not that she doesn't love him or that she isn't honoring him. She's seeing things from a different perspective and is moving on in life. He said to tell you that he's happy that she's moving on in life. She has not forgotten him at all. You know you were created with passion and love—it was a very heavenly space—and he had all hopes on you. And you are everything he ever wanted in a son—everything about you that he wanted in a son. Because you have had this experience, sweetheart, there is someone you will help not kill themselves and something that you will say that will help them. I just want you to know that.

"The words I heard are, 'It's better to take a risk than not at all. I am grateful. I am grateful.' He's crying right now, but they aren't only sad tears. They are happy tears, too. He said, 'I'm so grateful. Believe me when I tell you this. I love you. I love your mom. I love your sister. I love my family. I love you.' He said that you are more of a man than he can ever be. My aunt is telling me that they are pulling your father back. It's this weird thing that happens when the soul comes in and then starts pulling back.

"He's got a fine son, and you will find your way. When the time comes that you hold your own child in your arms, know that your father is the one who will be there, carrying your child into your arms. He's working behind the scenes. He said to tell you to be careful of politics. He's acknowledging that you are a great athlete, or he's saying that life is like a game. See what team you're on, what your strengths are, what your weaknesses are, and you go for that goal. Reach your goal.

"Shuffle the cards, honey," Lily said to Cory.

"Okay," Cory said.

"You are someone who is very, very brave. You have the courage to say what you are grateful for with your relationship with your father and other people you love. This is where the soul sees things for what they are and then lets them go. You realize that it's not your fault, right? Here's the thing. We all have to fail one way or another in order to succeed. So this is where the soul must be grateful for the things that didn't work out because on some level it helps you to take the higher road. You need that male bonding. You miss it. You need that one-on-one that only a dad can give you. I see this lack of abundance, and it doesn't mean material things. Tell me what it means."

171

"I live with my mom," Cory said, "and I used to live with my sister. I miss my dad so much, and I miss the time we spent together. Sometimes I get angry, and sometimes I get sad."

"If you ever decided to do any kind of coaching or mentoring, especially young males, I think it would be good for you," Lily said. "You want somebody to be the authority figure. You know what I mean? I understand that. You're missing the nurturing that comes from a man. That's what you're missing a lot—the nurturing that comes from a man. How about your friends, honey? How are they with you?"

"Not good."

"No one will ever replace your dad," Lily said. "That's the thing. You trusted him, and he trusted you. He still does. But you're grieving, and that's going to take a while. I don't think you're ever going to stop grieving your father—ever. My father crossed over when he was fifty-one, and I'll be fifty-one this year. And I think about how young that is and how much I miss him. Your path is to build your self-esteem and your self-worth at this time. Are you in a relationship with someone right now?"

"No," Cory said.

"It's kind of good that you're not. Your soul is grieving, and because of that, it needs to be by itself. It's very important for you to build your self-esteem. Now you graduated. Where did you graduate from?"

"High school."

"Where are you going from there?" Lily asked.

"Burlington. To college."

"Good for you. Good for you. Go all the way. You are seeing life as it really is. There is no illusion in your life anymore. You are in a state of total new beginnings. The slate has been wiped clean. You're going to go to Burlington. What is your passion? Is there something you really want to do?"

"It's helping people," Cory answered. "I want to either go into health care or be a teacher."

"I think that would be awesome," Lily said. "I just see you as a mentor. I really do. I see this image of you. You're older. And I see this kid, and he's never had a father figure in his life. They feel like they have a mother figure in their lives, but Mom doesn't know how to do certain things. And I see you as someone who says, 'Let me show you how to do this. Let's do this together.' Their gratitude will be enormous. Look at this. If you follow your passion, you will have success. But you're talking about investing six years of your time before that success will come. So from the time you start at Burlington, there's a six-year period where you'll focus on what will bring you great success. The thing is that when you're grieving, it's sometimes hard to focus. But that focus is going to make you very successful.

"This is interesting. There is a lot of past life stuff coming up. It tells me that in your last life—You see, sometimes we change roles, and I think your father could have been your son in another lifetime, and your mother could have been your daughter. You never know. This is a past life thing. I know that you can never kill love. It continues to grow. So I'm sure you will be together again at another time, if you so choose.

"Did you ever watch the movie *What Dreams May Come* with Robin Williams?"

"No."

"I'm going to give you a homework assignment to watch that movie. Look at this, though. You will walk the path of higher consciousness and understanding the things that are not just common. It's almost like unexplainable—That's beautiful. If you go at your own pace, you do much better. When someone has a lotus blossom in their cards, that means they've gone through something tough emotionally, and this is where it makes them more receptive to the good things in life. You'll see that you'll savor things, but you do need an outlet to express your feelings. Did you ever go through grief counseling at all?"

"I did."

"Did it help?"

"Not much."

"You still have a lot that's still there, a lot that's repressed, especially around special occasions—holidays, birthdays. You think about him and wish he was there. When you're thinking about him, he's thinking about you. Never doubt that. If you doubt that, it's going to cut off the flow of communication. You're thinking about him. He's thinking about you. Don't edit things. Don't edit your feelings with him. If something pissed you off, you need to tell him. That helps him to grow and heal on the other side, and it helps you. Honesty is the most important thing.

"I bet you're very, very aware of when you see other people with their fathers, and you can also see when they don't appreciate their fathers. You're very aware. This will help you with your success. It will help you to become more successful for many, many reasons. As a father too. You will be an awesome father, the most awesome father there is. Is there something you feel guilty about in regards to his crossing or in regards to your relationship?"

"I was the last person to talk to him. About forty-five minutes before it happened," Cory said. "I was on my way home. I've always felt guilty that if I had gotten there on time, if I had gotten there ten minutes early, maybe I could have stopped him."

"No, you couldn't have, honey. It was his choice. Do you remember what the conversation was about?"

"He called me and asked me where I was, and I told him I was dropping off my uncle's dog at my grandparents' house and then I was going to go home. And he said he wasn't going to be there when I got home. I asked why, and he said he was going for a drive. I thought he might be depressed and need to work some stuff out. When I got home, he wasn't there."

"Where did they find him, honey?"

"My grandparents' cottage garage. In a car."

"You know your grandparents' cottage had a lot of good memories, and it's kind of like returning to the womb, a place you think is safe and happy. I'm going to tell you exactly what I hear. He had thought about it over and over again. I don't care what anybody says. I don't know if he was taking antidepressants or if he had drunk something. I don't care what anyone says. When someone is that depressed, there are holes in their aura, and there are things out there that take advantage of that so they can destroy lives and destroy the good that's in there. The battle, sweetheart, is for you to say, 'I refuse,' because you tried so hard. Say, 'I'm not going to invest in that energy. I'm going to invest in the energy that was good between us, and I'm not going to let someone knock me down.' Because here's the thing. You must be pretty important, sweetheart. You must be very, very important. Because if we take him down, that will prevent a lot of hearts from healing. This is the hardest thing anyone can ever go through. I can't even imagine what you're going through. But I know this. You're worth it. Do you have any questions for me before I go, honey?"

"No."

"I hope on some level this is healing for the soul," Lily said. "I will tell you that he's in a peaceful place. He's in a very beautiful place. It's outdoors, and the air is clean and fresh. His soul is healing, and you will see him again—I guarantee it. You will see him again, and it will be wonderful. Take care of your soul, sweetheart."

"Thanks so much," Cory said.

"You're very welcome."

CHAPTER 28

Cory began his first semester at Burlington at the end of August. He felt closer to his father, who had once wandered the very same campus. Though far from whole, he was beginning to heal. Eva had graduated and found a job she liked. She was also engaged to Ian, her boyfriend. Charlie was thriving in San Francisco, where he was slowly learning to not worry so much about the rest of us. It felt like we were finally moving forward.

Yet I couldn't help feeling like I needed to talk to Lily again. Although I couldn't quite put a finger on it, I felt certain there was some unfinished business that needed tending to. I was glad Mark had told Cory that I was moving on and that it was okay. Cory and Eva both needed to understand that it was time for me to begin a new journey. It was hard for them to think about me having a life without their father, and I totally got that. Mark and I had been so close, so connected. But I couldn't stay in the same place forever.

"Is there something you want me to focus on?" Lily asked after I sat down for a one-on-one session with her.

"I've seen you before," I said, "and it's always been about my husband."

"I know," Lily replied.

"Now it's about me," I said.

"Can I just tell you what your energy is like right now? You remind me of a very satisfied cat who's purring. That's what your energy is like right now. When the soul purrs like that, it wants to be stroked. It wants to be petted. It wants to be touched. If you've ever watched cats, they are very regal. They let you touch them as long as *they* want, not as long as *you* want to. And when they're done with you, they walk away. That tells me a lot about your soul right now. This is about you and your satisfaction being first and foremost and being empowered in that and knowing that you have everything and more, draw in everything you want and truly desire. You can also say that you don't want that and don't want to participate in that."

"I've never been very good at that," I said.

"By the time you are done with the season, you're going to be a pro. And actually it will make you feel more attractive and be more attractive. Things will really be much better for you, and you're going to say to yourself, 'Why didn't I do this sooner?' You're really becoming empowered as to who you are, so your identity is evolving and shifting. And there are some things in the past that were safe for you, and now the soul is saying, 'I want to take a risk.' The thing is this is where the soul is acknowledging itself as the authority who can give herself permission to do what she wants to do and refuse to do what she doesn't want to do. So . . . from this deck, can you please choose six cards and place them facedown one on top of the other?"

I did as instructed.

"Good job," she said as she counted out the six cards. Then she handed the deck back to me. "I'd like you to select at least nine cards and place them down on top of each other."

Once I had finished, she counted out the cards again.

"Very good," she said. "From this deck, I need you to select eleven cards, and then you're going to place them on top of each other."

I heard the Tibetan bell again.

"You've given yourself permission to be a little risqué," Lily said. "I know I mentioned taking a risk, but the risqué can even border on a little bit of naughtiness."

I laughed.

"But it's perfect for your energy field. It's like you're alive. This is where you're saying, 'I am alive, and I feel. I'm not limited to one space and time. I'm ageless, and I'm timeless.' And so the soul is saying, 'I'm alive!' This is a really good energizing period for you. And there are some things that were taken for granted or became routine in the past, and now the soul is saying, 'I change that. Here's what works for me. I'm not going to settle for anything else.' It's really interesting. Sometimes we might put someone else's feelings ahead of our own, and when we do that, we do it for all the right reasons. Your soul said, 'I did everything for all the right reasons.' You were there. You were functioning, and you made it happen for everyone else. Now you needed to come off the shelf. Now this is where the soul is really enjoying and appreciating some of the things that were put on the back burner or that you just never had the chance to appreciate it. You're in a good space, honey bear.

"There's an eagle that's holding on to an actual rattlesnake. The eagle is always the great teacher. The eagle is always the leader. This is about the choices you're making. It's not only for your benefit, but it will also be healing for those around you, even those you have not met yet. Your journey is going to help them have hope and to come back alive. And so the thing is, the more raw and unedited you are, the more feeling will manifest. I don't know how to explain that except to say that this is not time for any illusions. This is just how it is. You may want to cover the stuff that is ugly and stinky. It's kind of like I don't like to make number two when there are other people around. I just don't want them to smell me. But actually I feel better afterward, and you flush it down. Who doesn't make a stink when it comes out? I don't know anyone who makes candy. This is about being honest with people and saying, 'Yeah, I fart.' If you go to the bathroom, do you focus on it all day? The rest of the day is not about what happened on that toilet. So that's what they're trying to tell me. Some people, even in your own family, have given themselves permission to show how they are fixing things and how everything is together."

Lily rang the Tibetan bell again, and I thought about what she had just said. She really had quite a sense of humor.

"I want you to take pictures. I want you to take photos. I just want you to take images of yourself. I mean, just really. If somebody has a camera, I want you to be in front of that camera, posing like you're a supermodel. Okay? You are going to see some of the happiest photos of your life. You are going to see some of the prettiest photos of your life. You are going to see yourself and think, *Oh, my God*. If you compare those pictures to how you felt three years ago, you're going to think that it's a miracle. The reason I'm telling you this is to acknowledge the miracle that you are, acknowledge how much you have blossomed. You had a choice in the matter."

The bell rang again, its chime a familiar and comforting sound.

"Don't wait for the egg that has never been hatched," Lily said. "Meaning if it looks like a chicken, it doesn't mean it's a real chicken. And it's like somebody waiting for the chicken to lay an egg, but it's not even laying an egg because it's not real. So watch out for those who are phony who keep telling you that the egg is coming, but it never does. See it for what it is. Because believe it or not, you are in a rooster position, and the rooster is the one who makes certain those eggs are going to be fertilized. You help things grow . . . bigger . . . better. Anyone who is attracted to you at this time had better not be a fake-ass chicken. Roosters tell you when it's time, and they give you early warning. If you're on a farm, that rooster is letting you know what's up before the sun is. You have your own internal alarm system that's going to let you know when someone's the real deal and when someone isn't.

"There are some people who are a little freaky and would like that fake chicken 'cause I've seen dogs hump stuffed animals. But you're looking for the real thing. You know that song, 'Ain't Nothing

Like the Real Thing, Baby'? That's what you're looking for. How are you going to find the real thing? Usually if I want to find out if pearls are real or not, I take them between my teeth. And if they're rough, they're real. If they're smooth, they're fake. Forget about it. Fake has purpose, but it usually doesn't last as long as the real thing. A genuine and authentic means a lot, and the thing is that right now you are being genuine and authentic. You are recognizing the original that you are."

More bells.

"Sometimes when people talk about Christmas and they talk about Mary on the donkey, they say, 'Oh, my God. Mary was carrying Jesus, who was supposed to be the Son of God, and she's on a donkey.' But what people don't realize is that back in the day, having a donkey was like having a Cadillac. That was like the best that there could be. Well, I closed my eyes and saw this image of you on a donkey, and I saw a man leading the donkey. He was really being careful and wanted to really make sure you were comfortable when you went over the bumps. You seemed like you were just having a great time because he's treating you like a princess."

I laughed.

"It's like he's taking the lead. You don't have to do anything. He will do it for you. That's how you know what true love is. He'll just know what you want. And he's just going to do it because he wants to please you. It's interesting right now because you're the dealer, and there's more than one person playing the game. So you have the possibility of having several players come into your life. You are the one who deals out the cards, so I wouldn't be surprised if there's more than one love interest manifesting at once. The interesting thing is that everybody wants to win, and they're sitting at your table for a reason. Part of you already knows which ones are going to cheat and which ones are really good card players.

"Now the throat chakra is very fascinating to me because that's where people come in again. Because that means you are actually communicating and are helping people to move forward. And you are going to find that if they really want to move forward, they will have to communicate, deal with the past. It has to come out so they can move forward. Sometimes the soul will grieve things it thinks it will never experience again. The thing is this individual is irreplaceable. The experience with that individual can never be duplicated. But that doesn't limit the playing field. It's kind of like a radio station. There are many stations to choose from, and they are all broadcasting right now. Which one are you going to receive? If you don't like what you hear, you change the channel. Before, you had made a commitment, and you said you were going to be the best you possibly could be. But you're in the gold chapter right now, and that means empowerment.

"The heart chakra is the center of love." Lily paused momentarily. "Did you see the movie *Ghost* before? It seems like an image from that movie—I don't know if this is an actual part of the movie or if I've just seen it this way. Remember when Patrick Swayze put his head up to the door when he was trying to make her understand that he was there, and she kind of feels it? Do you know what I'm talking about? That's your heart. You are still communicating with someone on the other side."

"My husband still wants to communicate," I said.

"Your husband wants to get through the door. It's like, 'I just want to talk to you.' Part of you says, 'I know you're there.' But it reminds me of when you're having a really incredible moment and the phone rings, and you don't want to answer it because you want to hold on to what's happening to you now. 'Honey, I know you're there. Go back to bed. I'm fine. I just want to be alone in my space.' So there is grief that's happening on the other side. It's painful for him, but at the same time he knows it's the right thing. He says that if he hadn't done what he did and crossed over, you and he would be enjoying this. But there were other things that began to become more important in your relationship. He says he feels very foolish because of that wasted time. It also tells him that either on the other side or in another lifetime he would want to do better. He would want to have a better experience. In other word he would make you his first priority. When the kids came, they became the priority. Work became the priority. You held it all together perfectly. What's really interesting is that you're seeing yourself clearly, and what you're saying is, 'Damn, girl.' One time I heard this song on my friend's phone that went something like, 'Damn, you're a sexy bitch.' I asked him, 'What the heck kind of song is that?' To me that's basically what your solar plexus is saying. It's saying, 'I'm really sexy. I'm beautiful, and I have it together.' You're going to notice that people are drawn to you and that they want to touch you because your light is really bright. You feel wonderful."

"Yes," I said. "All I want to do is giggle."

"You're going to have paparazzi—people who want to know what you're wearing and what you're doing. What's the secret? They are going to want to know why you have this energy. People are going to want to know because it may be very foreign to what their experience is. That's a really great gift to humanity because it gives them hope again. I love that about you.

"In the solar plexus . . . I don't know what you have planned, sweetheart, but you're going to go on a nice little trip with your kids where you're going to do something with them. I know they have holidays like Thanksgiving and Easter, but this is a time when the soul says, 'Anytime we get to spend together is a holiday.' And it doesn't have to be around Thanksgiving or Christmas. That's important to you. The time you spend is very important. I notice that your children, especially when they come home after a trip, may have a melancholy moment because tied to that may be that sad news is waiting for us.

"So I'm going to give you a homework assignment, and this is going to take some doing on your part. Upon their arrival I would like there to be some sort of gift waiting for them, something they would absolutely love. It could be a wrapped gift with a card from you that says how much you love them and appreciate them. So you can shift the energy of the trauma. Understand? They come home to something wonderful and are amazed by how you were able to do it and plan it. That's a cool thing. I actually see you doing it, and I see how touched they are. You'll know exactly what to do too, and you'll do a great job. Creativity is everything, and you score points for the expressions of love.

"Just below the navel in the expressions of passion and creativity, you're—*whoa!* What? Well, that's fabulous. I have to tell you that there's a huge frog that's very feminine-looking. Frogs are major transformations and changes. Once you sat on that lily pad for a little while, you saw what you wanted, and you just went for it. Have you ever seen a frog go for something?"

I giggled again.

"They go fast. They surprise me because you'd think they would go real fast, but they don't. They just—*boom!* This is a satisfied mama frog, and she kind of reminds me of—'Wow, I've been busted. I've been busted.' It's interesting that the lily pad she's sitting on is golden. And there's a lot of croaking around her, which means there are many who want to mate with her, and she's just kind of taking it all in. So that's beautiful.

"I'm going to say this without a shadow of a doubt. I believe that your happiest days are yet to come. Some of them are going to be wonderful, really cool."

Chapter 29

"What was your purpose in coming here this time?" Lily asked.

"I still tend to go back to the way I used to be," I answered. "Me in this new life now, I want things to change. I'm ready. I'm energized. And I still get stuck in the tragedy. Not as much. I don't want to be like that person was. I'm writing about it. I'm telling the story. And I've helped other people already."

"I know you have," Lily said.

"I help souls in my dreams."

"That's very real."

"It is very real," I said. "That was another reason I wanted to come. Because I needed that affirmation. I tend to vibrate very high now."

"For you to be at that level now is very powerful. It means that the divine has a greater purpose for you, and you're the best candidate to help those who are between realms."

"I feel that," I said.

"You need to acknowledge yourself and your abilities. People in your dreams have not necessarily crossed over. Some of them may be stuck."

"I know."

"Yes. Some of them may be here in this realm and sleeping and appearing to you in your dreams. The only caution I have for you is that if you ever wake up feeling exhausted, I want you to make sure you take a bath in some lavender or rose oil and just allow yourself to soak. Okay? Yes, it's very real. When you start having people you have never met before in your dreams and they tell you that you are helping them, don't be surprised.

"You have a choice when stuff like this happens. Some people fall into all different identities when they experience a tragedy. But your soul made a choice, and you said you felt it to the core of your very being. You felt it. You experienced it, and it almost killed you. Then there came a time when the soul said, 'I'm ready to live again.' Now there's so much healing that's happening. It's really amazing. And when you fall back into the tragedy, it's okay. Because every time you do it, it's a little less. The thing is that if you had been the person you are now and this tragedy was manifesting, it would not turn out as well as it is going to turn out. The best is yet to come."

"I feel that," I said.

"And your soul has a purpose. Your soul had a divine calling, and you don't have to feel pressured and don't have to put in a full forty-hour week. The moment it happens, you'll know it, and you'll just flow with it. Have you ever watched a show called *Touch by an Angel*? That's like the character you will be if you choose to be. Every time you think you're taking a break and a vacation, someone is going to show up that really does need the assistance that you can provide. Sometimes you won't know who it is. And at other times they'll contact you, and you will know. You're holy right now. You're a holy vessel. That's a reminder to you to always keep who you are sacred and safe. Don't let anyone or anything violate your sacred temple. That doesn't mean you have to be perfect because that imperfection is celebrated. So even the things you think might have been mistakes were actually the right way to go." Lily paused a moment. "Do you have any questions for me?"

"I tend to pick up on negative thoughts from people," I said, "especially from my husband's family."

"I have the answer. I have to tell you something. As soon as you started talking about your husband's family, all the lights in your energy field were turned off. It was like you were this beautiful shining star, and then it was gone. Now why would you see them for the holidays? Give them a gift certificate for a restaurant and be done with it."

"Those are my kids' grandparents," I said. "But nothing good ever comes of it—ever."

"So what are the plans?"

"Quick day," I said. "No overnight. Just a quick dinner."

"Good," Lily said. "Okay, let's back up the train a little bit and start from the very beginning of this session. You have a choice."

"I know."

"This is where you can say that you have the right to make your own decisions. 'My identity as his wife is done, so my identity now is *no*. This doesn't work out for me. I've made other plans.' If the children want to go, you can drop them off. I know you like to spend time with your kids, but . . . *jeez*."

"That whole obligation," I said, "all that stuff is over. I really don't talk to my in-laws much anymore. Every time I see them, I feel awful afterward."

"I don't know where you are financially, but I've been in this business for well over a decade. And I've tried all kinds of things because the brighter your light is, the more attracted people are to you. The thing that works for me the best is *mendal mognola*. It's called 'the wheel of light.' It went through all kinds of scientific testing before it proved to fortify your aura and protect you. Now I have the battle with what are considered to be evil people a lot."

"I know," I said. "So did my husband."

"They're ugly," Lily said. "Since I put this on, I have had very little problems. I've always wanted a solid gold one, but it's three thousand dollars. And it's supposed to amplify you more than this one. But this one does the job. It's sterling silver, and in the center is emerald. It costs about a 150 dollars and would be good for you to have. I'm telling you as a magical being everyone who gets one notices that things that used to bother them don't bother them anymore. No matter how people act, it doesn't even infiltrate. So what was the question again?"

"I don't remember."

"I went off on a tangent," Lily said.

"That's okay," I said. "It was just dealing with stuff, and I'm very sensitive."

"Yes. The thing is, too, that in this lifetime the approval of others has been very important to you. And the thing you need to do is know that you've already passed the test and you don't have to do anything more with this family."

I couldn't help laughing. It felt great.

"You don't have to prove anything," Lily said. "I think it's beautiful the way you've handled this. The thing is it gives them a false sense that everything is okay. Do you understand what I'm saying? But this is also important to those who are on the other side. They enjoy watching everyone interact. It's time now to move on. Remember when I told you about being a little bit naughty and about taking a risk? There's something in you that tells me that you don't care how they react or respond."

"I'm free," I said.

"Someone is going to look at you and say, 'Man, I always wanted to say that.' I mean, you aren't going to be disrespectful. Maybe you're going to actually be respectful of yourself this time."

"I always wondered how the separation I've created affected Mark on the other side," I said, "because we're not a part of that family anymore."

"You're happier that way."

"I know I am."

"If you could have done this sooner with him alive," Lily said, "you would have."

"I would have," I said. "If I had pushed that harder—"

"You were everything," Lily began before she changed directions. "I still consider you to be perfection," Mark said. "You were his sanity from an insane family, and he says he's so glad 'our kids aren't like that.'"

"They're not," I said. "They're not like that because of me."

"That's true," Lily said. "He just put a crown on your head and is acknowledging you. So . . . what was the question again?"

I giggled. "I need to trust who I am, and I need to trust that feeling."

"Trust yourself," Lily said.

"It's really important," I said.

"It's okay to say to someone, 'We're not going to be able to attend.' Of course they're going to be disappointed. Don't disappoint yourself anymore. You know, since the kids are involved, ask them and tell them this is how you really feel."

"I do," I said.

"When kids are little, you know how sometimes we make them do stuff, and we make them hug people they don't really want to hug? Well, that's something adults don't have to do."

Lily turned over another card. "Look at this," she said. "Forgiveness. Courage—"

"Forgiveness is huge," I said.

"Yes," Lily agreed. "This is interesting because forgiveness fuels your courage to reach expressions of love. You felt very abandoned when that decision was made."

"God, yes," I said.

"It affected your self-worth, but you also recognized where you abandoned your own self-worth. Look at this surrender card. I just had to see it as it was. 'I'm not quitting. I just surrender.'"

"Perfect," I said, still laughing.

"How many times do you have to keep talking about it? You see it for what it really is. Thank you for not abandoning the trauma. You'll abandon so-and-so, but you won't abandon that hurt. You hold on to it. This is where you're saying, 'I'm not going to do that anymore. I'm not going to hold on to that pain and hurt. I'm not going to allow them to do that to me because that's not who I am.' It's okay for you to say, 'I don't feel comfortable when you say this or do that.' I bet they'll think about what you said next time. It also brought up another one of your fears—that maybe no one wants to commit to you for the rest of their life. You also aren't sure if you want to be with someone for the rest of your life. The fear of commitment. Because you had to examine what it is that you were committed to, the relationship you were in, and whether that commitment was real or an illusion. This is so deep. I wish we had five hours together because I have so much information for you. It's amazing. You need to have faith. You know what I love? Faith in yourself."

"I'm special," I said.

"You are. If anyone doubts you, they can look at your light. As soon as you stop talking about his family, your light becomes so bright again. Okay?"

"So true."

"Just say, 'Lily looked at me and said I have the divine power, and I am special.' Faith—even when you feel like something happened beyond your control. To have faith—even during those types of moments. All of a sudden your aura is filled with a stream of beautiful balloons."

"I felt them."

"They just went up in the air. It was so cool. Do you know what color those balloons were? They were pearl-colored. And that always means that 'I went through something difficult, but I got through it.' So . . . that's wonderful."

Lily studied another card. "There's a theme—commitment. I know you're committed to your children, and I know that you're committed to yourself. You're someone who sees beyond those illusions. That knight in shining armor wasn't really a knight in shining armor. Love is coming. You just draw it in. Someone who's been drawn to you has also gone through some sort of heartache or tragedy, or they've been a victim of something. This is why you'll be brought together—to laugh. You're giving yourself permission to laugh, laugh from the belly so hard that you can't stop laughing. This would be good for you. So comedy, things that make you laugh, would be good for you." Lily put the cards down. "We have about two minutes. Do you have any questions?"

"I have one," I said. "My mother's dying, and I always wonder when she's leaving and what she's experiencing. She's struggling with her faith and what's going to happen next, and I've been trying to calm her. But I'm failing."

"Honey, can I tell you about your mom? It's like somebody lying in bed. Remember Granny on the *Beverly Hillbillies*? She's lying on the bed."

"Exactly."

"'Oh, I can't do anything.' As long as she's like that, she's going to stick around. She likes the news. Give her something to talk about because that keeps her going. But if you don't want that—"

"She's so angry," I said, interrupting Lily, "because she's in bed and her body is failing."

"Can I tell you that there's also a part of her that feels that when she was young and youthful she devoted her life to her family? And the reward was that when she got older she would be able to enjoy some of that. And she kind of has some regrets. There were identities that she filled for people around her that aren't who she truly is. She's clearing that so that when she comes back she's not going to limit herself. She's going to challenge people's expectations and do what she expects of herself. This is going to be huge for her, so I'm actually glad she's in that situation. When she finally figures out that she already knows what's going to happen and is at peace, she will cross over." Lily paused. "You're in the process of creating—I'm sorry."

"I'm writing the story," I offered.

"You're on an adventure, and this is where the soul is trusting and letting go."

"My sister called me Sybil," I said.

"Well, if she saw what I saw with the change in your aura—"

"She said that I have veils that come over my face," I explained.

"You do. That's like your energy field, and your husband's family drains you. They're like vampires. Part of your soul is saying, 'Don't do it now.' You have a choice, and these are your choices. You can do whatever makes everyone else happy, which will contribute to your own sorrow, or you can say you've come full circle. 'I'm mature, and I'm going to say it like it is. And that's all there is to say.'" Lily glanced at another card. "Look at this. 'I have some journeys to go on. I'm going to go somewhere.' The traveling rebel."

"Oh," I said.

"Whoa. Okay. It helps you to see things clearly beyond. And that's what I would say to you. Stick with the issue and not what's projected at you. The soul is being told, 'Stop putting off your happiness. I'm ready for a gold medallion. I'm ready for it. But that's because I'm choosing better for myself. I'm choosing the best.' And that's what these cards say. So what will you choose—expression or suppression? This is where the soul says, 'I'm a volcano, and I have to erupt.' So . . . there you go. It's a great time for you."

CHAPTER 30

*A*fter Cory left for college in August, I was relieved, sad, and lonely, and I wasn't sure what my next move was going to be. I had no idea who I was when I wasn't dealing with Mark or Cory's issues, and I needed to find that out. It was time for me to take a good look at myself and find out who Kandace really was. I also wanted to spend more time with my mother, who was bedridden and dying. I knew that I wouldn't return to the workforce until after she had passed away.

One thing I had been trying to do since Mark's death was pay attention to the signs. I got another chance to do exactly that when a woman named Paula called me while I was visiting Charlie, my oldest son, in California. Paula, a recruiter, was recruiting for a human resources manager position for a company in Burlington, although she was working through their Montpelier office. My old boss from the Burlington rec center was interviewing for the job and had listed me as a reference. As Paula and I talked, she said she was thinking about starting a recruiting business. She suggested that maybe I'd be interested in working for her.

"After you get back to Montpelier," she said, "give me a call."

I did just that, and we set up a meeting. I brought my resume, and she brought hers. But instead of talking about her potential business startup, we began to talk a little bit about life.

"Let me tell you what I've been through," Paula said. She went on to tell me about her recent divorce among other things.

When she was finished, I shared my story about Mark's suicide, and as I spoke, I saw the expression on her face change.

"Oh, my God," she said.

"What?" I asked.

"We weren't supposed to meet about a job at all," she said. "I prayed last night for God to help me find a way to help my friend, Barbara, who lost her sister to suicide. You're it."

We ended up talking for two hours about what had happened to Barbara's sister and what had brought us together.

"When did Barbara's sister die?" I asked.

"October 13th," Paula answered.

My mouth dropped opened. "That's my birthday."

I was rocked with chills. This was no coincidence that we had been brought together. I had work to do. I recalled all the important signs I had received on my birthday—my sister's coworker telling her about Lily on my birthday, going to see Lily with my daughter the next year on my birthday, and now this.

She gave me Barbara's number, but before I could call Barbara, my mother took a turn for the worse. Her heart was in constant atrial fibrillation, which meant she was at risk for a stroke or a heart attack. She'd already had some minor strokes, leaving her weak on her left side. Once she had become bedridden, her condition had slowly deteriorated. After eight months in bed her organs were beginning to shut down.

She was dying. I talked to her all the time about what was happening to her. Her mind was still sharp, so she understood everything that was going on. She would talk to me about her fears. I had made a commitment to spend this final time with her and to help her in any way I could.

With Cory away at school I settled into a routine with Lizzy, who also wanted to be with Mom as often as possible. We would meet in West Castleton, where my mom's assisted living facility was located, and talk over a sandwich and a beer. Then we would go spend time at our mother's bedside. Mom could engage in conversation, and she was still engaged in the lives of all her kids. As long as she was still connected, she wasn't going anywhere soon. She hadn't let go of her family. She still wanted to keep up with the family gossip. Lily had also said she was doing a lot of soul searching, an important part of her final journey. My mother's soul was coming to terms with what she had and hadn't done in this lifetime. She was making peace with it. As Lily had taught me, you take it all with you. It's not a free pass when you die.

Her journey toward her final sunset was not always calm or pleasant. Sometimes she became agitated and scared and didn't want to let go. She said on several occasions that she had been hovering above her body and looking down at it.

"I was looking down at myself," she would say, "and then I got back into my body."

I told her that she was practicing leaving. Her soul was beginning to let go. I tried to explain to her that dying didn't hurt. She was afraid of the pain associated with it. But I told her repeatedly that it would be a little disorienting at first but then she would be so glad to be out of that body.

"You will run and leap toward the light," I said, "and you will be so happy."

She wanted to believe me. "How do you know this?" she kept asking.

"I don't know," I would answer. "I just do."

I had to laugh one day when she was talking to my sister and asked, "Do you think I will come back as one of Kandace's ghosts?"

"You won't be a ghost," I said. "You'll be a spirit. You've done all your soul searching here for the last eight months. You're going to go where your soul is supposed to go, without lingering. When you see Mark, choke him for me."

She laughed heartily. Then the smile disappeared from her face. "I never understood how he could leave you and the kids—never. When I see him, I'll tell him."

Her time to go finally arrived on a cold January day. Most of us kids were there. I had volunteered for the night shift since I had the fewest obligations. That afternoon and early evening we took shifts at her bedside. Her breathing was labored. The death rattle had settled in. I talked with her some, making sure to touch her so she knew she wasn't alone.

She would open her eyes periodically and say a few words. "I love you. I'm so thankful for all of you."

I pulled out the manuscript I had been working on and showed it to her.

She didn't say anything, but a big smile spread across her face.

I bent down and kissed her on the cheek. "We're going to go eat dinner, Mom. We'll be back."

A group of us drove to a nearby pub, which was owned by an old high school friend of mine by the name of Nathan. This was where Lizzy and I did most of our talking when we were in town to visit Mom.

Dave, my second oldest brother, said he would stay to look after Mom during dinner. Then I would return for the night shift, while the others went home for the day.

At the local pub we ordered our food and then started sharing stories from our childhood. Everyone had a favorite moment with Mom and was eager to share. Kevin, my third oldest brother, laughed harder than I'd ever seen him laugh.

Then Lynn, Kevin's daughter and my niece, looked down at her cell phone, which was vibrating. Kevin looked at his. He'd missed a call. Likewise, when I glanced at mine, I saw that I'd missed a call from Lizzy's phone.

We all looked at Lizzy.

"I don't have my phone with me," she said as soon as she realized it.

Then it hit us. Mom had died. Dave had been using Lizzy's phone to try to contact us.

Lynn handed her phone to Lizzy.

She listened a moment and then shared the news from Dave. "Mom just took her last breath."

We jumped up and ran out the door but not before we remembered to quickly pay the bill. I pulled the car around, and in less than five minutes, we were standing at Mom's bedside, staring at a shell that no longer contained life. It was as if she had bolted from that body, finally set free.

"I felt her leave," Dave said. He had felt a moment of love and gratitude before she flew out of there.

We said our good-byes, which was weird, because I knew she wasn't there anymore. Then Lynn and I helped the funeral director bag up her crippled body and walked with her down to the van. I zipped the bag over her head before she was put in the van. It felt like the most normal thing in the world—not strange or morbid but comforting and calming.

We spent the next few days planning the funeral, and during that time we opened a package Mom had left for us with a letter, a few favorite psalms, quotes, and so on. I read one of them and realized it summed up not only my mom's life but also my own. I told my siblings I had to read it at the funeral. It was important to me.

> After a while, you learn the subtle difference between holding a hand and chaining a soul. And you learn that love doesn't mean leaning and company doesn't mean security. And you begin to understand that kisses aren't contracts and presents aren't promises. And you begin to accept your defeats with your head held high and your eyes open, with the grace of a woman, not the grief of a child. You learn to build your roads on today, because tomorrow's ground is too uncertain, and futures have a way of falling down in mid-flight. After a while, you learn that even sunshine burns if you get too much. So

you plant your own garden and decorate your own soul,
instead of waiting for someone to bring you flowers. And
you learn that you really can endure, that you really are
strong. And that you really do have worth and that you
keep learning. With every goodbye, you learn—

At the bottom of the page my mom wrote, "This is pretty much
the story of my life. Good-bye, my darlings."

While I was reading those words at the funeral, surrounded by
my sisters, I felt Mom's soul wrap itself around me. My legs began
to shake. I had a hard time standing, so my sisters grabbed me and
held on to me while I finished. I then took my seat, and all I felt was
the love, the overwhelming love that was my mom.

───────

How do people find their way after their purpose is gone? I was
lost. I needed to make some changes, but I felt paralyzed. One of
the reasons I had moved to Middleburg was to help my mom, and I
hadn't really done anything else. I hadn't looked for a job or thought
about what I was going to do in the future. Now that she was gone,
I felt out of sorts, not really knowing what to do. I was down and
grew depressed. Moving to Middleburg and quitting my other job
began to haunt me.

My mother had given me something to do besides grieve Mark's
death. I hadn't had to look at myself or the terrible things I had been
through. I had been able to focus on her and worry about her. After
her death I knew it was time to move and cut my expenses. It was
time to get a job and improve my life, but I had no idea how to do
either. I became anxious. I didn't know if I should move closer to
Jack and see if I could make that work. If I took a job in town and
then moved, how would that work? I was unable to make any sort
of decision.

A couple weeks after Mom's death, I got in touch with Barbara, Paula's friend who had lost a sister to suicide. We met for lunch at an Italian restaurant, and even though I had never met her before, I felt as though I had known her forever. We gave each other a big hug and then sat down.

"Let me tell you a little bit about what happened," she said.

Her sister had died just two months earlier on October 13, my birthday. I knew right then that we had been brought together for a reason and that this wasn't a coincidence. After we told each other our stories, we ate lunch and then said good-bye. Maybe I had a purpose after all.

CHAPTER 31

I was on my way home after lunch with Barbara when I got a call from Jessica, an old friend and former roommate. Jessica and I had been friends since I'd first moved to Burlington in 1980. She had even been one of my bridesmaids at my wedding. We could almost be mistaken for twins—same height, weight, build, and hair color. But while I had brown eyes, hers were a beautiful hazel green. We drifted apart now and then, depending on what was going on in our lives, but we always managed to find our way back to each other.

At the moment she wanted to know if I could talk to her sister-in-law and help her and her son deal with the suicide of her ex-husband. I was once again rocked with chills. What was happening? Why were these people being guided to me? Was this God's way of telling me what my new purpose was going to be? Everything Lily had said was coming true, and it was happening on the heels of Mom's death. It seemed to me that now was the time for me to start living my soul's purpose.

A couple of days later I left for Burlington. I had to meet with my financial advisor and pick up my taxes. I also had to meet with Jenny, who was going to mentor me on possibly going into business for myself. She had mentored me previously when I had lived in the apartment in Burlington. She was my age, in her middle fifties, and she had short light brown hair, blue eyes, and a friendly demeanor. Shortly before Mark's death Mark and I had talked about opening a furniture consignment shop together. He started a file for it, naming it "Coming Home." After his death and after Cory and I had moved into the apartment, I had been shopping in Burlington when I stumbled upon a furniture consignment shop named "Coming Home." Briefly frozen in disbelief, I had been certain it was a sign. I'd gone in and met Jenny, the owner, and we became friends. She went on to help me furnish the apartment, but more importantly she was there for me and often let me visit when I simply needed silent company.

Now here she was again in my life. Although I planned to stay overnight with Jessica, my first stop after meeting with my financial advisor was dinner with Jenny. We met for dinner to talk about opening a business, but we never did talk shop. Instead, we talked about how she could help her daughter, who she believed was on the verge of drinking herself to death.

"At what point do I realize I can't help her anymore?" she asked.

As she spoke, it slowly dawned on me that I hadn't been guided to Jenny so she could help me learn how to open a business. I had been guided to her so I could help her with her daughter.

The next day after a late-night chat with Jessica and her husband, I found myself drawn to stop in at the rec center, where I had once worked. Once inside I wandered upstairs to meet the woman who had taken over my position. She was in her thirties and had short dark brown hair and a somewhat heavyset build. She was walking the treadmill when I met her and was sweaty and out of breath. I felt bad for interrupting her workout, but she was gracious.

"It hasn't been easy filling your shoes," she said.

On my way out I ran into Kathy, an old friend from high school who lived in Burlington. She had spent some time with me after Mark had died and had been very supportive. (She had been with me at the hockey rink the night Cory blew out his right knee.) She ran over to me and gave me a big hug.

Then she stepped back and looked at me. "You know, you have a bright light around you," she said.

I laughed. I hadn't showered or even washed my hair that morning. I knew right then and there that I had been touched by something way bigger than anything I had ever imagined. I had a purpose from the divine, from God.

I walked out to my car, got in, and noticed I had several missed calls on my cell from Barbara, the woman who had lost her sister to suicide. "Call me," she said in a message on my voice mail. "It's urgent."

I dialed her number, and Barbara immediately filled me in on what she had learned since I'd last spoken with her.

"Oh, my God, Kandace," she said. "My sister didn't kill herself. She was murdered by her husband."

There was a reason I had been pulled into this. As had been the case with Katherine's husband, an apparent suicide no longer looked like suicide. *Here we go again*, I thought. I spent the next several weeks helping Barbara's family however I could. We organized a team of people who had been clearly brought together by her sister's spirit.

I was also trying to figure out my next move. Should I move out of the big house in Middleburg? I had a job interview set up at a college in Montpelier. *Should I go back to work?* I wondered, *or move closer to Jack, a man I was crazy about?* I was out of sorts.

A few nights later my mom came and talked to me in a visitation dream. "You're a very good daughter," she told me, "and I love you very much. You were always so good to me. You were right. They are all here—the Father, Son, and Holy Spirit."

She also said that I had a gift and would help many people but that I needed to move out of the big house, take the job, settle my soul, and get into a comfortable dance where I knew all the steps. It was important for my soul to be settled so I could learn. She said I was in school now. She also said Jack loved me very much. He was conflicted but would make a choice, and he would be devastated if he had to give me up. I would take a trip with him soon, and then I would know. I wasn't sure what I was supposed to know, but I would find out later.

"You should write the book," she said. She shook her finger at me. "It's important. It will help many people and have an effect on your family's finances for generations to come."

She told me that I would speak in front of people and that I would have an outline but that I would always set the outline down and speak from my heart. She said I would write two books. Then she said she had spoken with Mark and had told him she didn't understand how he could leave his family. She said it would be a long time before he forgave himself. I already knew that to be true.

CHAPTER 32

hen the day of my job interview at the college arrived, I couldn't help but marvel at my good fortune. I had stumbled upon a tiny ad in the newspaper, an ad that had only run one day, and now here I was about to interview for the position of evening education coordinator at the college. The interview went well—so well that the small staff of three knew the instant I walked through the door that I was the one—and two hours later they called and offered me the position.

Not long after that Cory and I were making a run to the donation center. (I was busily cleaning out our house in anticipation of moving.) Then I got a call from Rich, a gentleman in New York who owned a duplex that I had inquired about. I had been looking for a place for a while now and had sent out a bunch of e-mails. So far I'd yet to find anything I liked. The places I had looked at had either been too small or in undesirable neighborhoods.

"I'm calling about the duplex in Shadow Crest," he said.

"Can you refresh my memory?" I asked.

"It was all in the ad."

"I'm driving right now," I said, "and I don't have the ad in front of me. Can I call you back?"

"Sure."

I forgot to call Rich back until the next day. But when I called, he was friendly and told me about the duplex, which he had built for his parents before his father had passed away. Now his mother lived on one side, but the other side was empty.

"Just go and take a look at it," he said. "Just give it a chance."

"Okay." I didn't even know where Shadow Crest was. I had never heard of it.

Rich told me he would have Dan, his brother-in-law, set up a time for me to look at the place.

Half an hour later my phone rang. It was Dan.

"I can look at it today at four," I said.

I entered the address into my GPS, and twenty minutes later I was there. Shadow Crest, a sleepy little bedroom community, was roughly seven miles west of Montpelier, much closer than I'd imagined. Situated in a valley surrounded by large bluffs, it had a grocery store, a coffee shop, a dry cleaner, a hardware store, and a variety of pubs. It was quite lovely. I later learned it was known for its hiking and biking trails.

The duplex appeared to have been built in the 1980s. It sat on a hill and looked more like a single-family residence than a two-family duplex. I liked that about it. Although it had been updated, it retained some older flooring and wall coverings, making it feel slightly retro. The unit I viewed had two bedrooms, one and a half baths, a living room, a dining room, and a kitchen. A small foyer greeted us as we entered. I liked how bright it was, with yellow paint, white woodwork, and white kitchen cabinets. It had good energy.

It seemed safe and secure and had a huge basement, which meant I wouldn't have to get rid of all my things if I moved in. There was something else too—a feeling I had that I was supposed to be there. I had no idea why I needed to be in Shadow Crest. The only thing I knew was that I needed to find a place, and it had to be easy.

I would learn later that after I left Dan called Rich in New York and told him, "She's the one." That was twice in one week that I'd had that effect on someone, first in my job interview and now while I was taking a look at the duplex.

Then Rich called me from New York.

"Sit down, Kandace," he said, perhaps sensing my anxiety. "You have a place to live. I don't need anything from you. We'll take care of the paperwork in due time."

I told him I was starting a new job and was stressed because I didn't know whether I wanted to go forward with it or move to Arizona. I was overwhelmed.

"Just start your new job and get settled in," he said. "Then we can take care of the details."

"That will work out just fine for me," I said.

I was astonished that he didn't want anything from me—not an application fee, not a security deposit, nothing. At every other place I'd looked, the process had been competitive. You had to prove your income, hurriedly fill out an application, and hope no one else snagged it first. As if fretting about moving wasn't stressful enough. But Rich trusted me. My word was enough. Things like that never happened in Montpelier, but I was moving into a smaller town. *Maybe things are different in Shadow Crest,* I thought. I had been crying all the time because I didn't want to move, even though I knew it was the wise thing to do. Now this place had just fallen into my lap. I'm certain now I was supposed to meet Rich. He helped settle me that day.

I went ahead and started my new job, and a few days later Rich told me he would meet with me on Easter when he was in town visiting his mother.

"I'm going to send you the paperwork," he said, "and you can just bring it with you."

Before I signed anything, I came back to look at the place again, this time with Rich showing me around. An interior designer in his fifties, he was tall and attractive, but his chain-smoking distracted from his good looks. I liked him right from the start. I offered to pay the rent for a year. Then we negotiated, and he reduced the rent by two hundred dollars a month. That was important to me. I had a certain amount I wanted to pay each month, and I didn't want to pay any more.

"I'll pay this for a year," I said as he took me through the basement.

"Done," he said.

"What about a security deposit?" I asked.

"Well, I don't need one."

I started up the basement steps and then stopped and turned toward him. "So, Rich," I began, "tell me what my references have said about me."

All I heard was silence.

"You did check my references, didn't you?"

"No."

I laughed. I knew I was supposed to live here.

I gave notice on the big house that no longer served its purpose. Eva was renting a house with her fiancé. Cory was planning to rent a house at school and live there starting in June, and Charlie was living his life in San Francisco. It was my time now. I needed to create a space for me, a space with good energy where I could focus on my new purpose and grow my gift. It was about me.

After I'd been at my new job for a few weeks, the director told me there was some bad stuff in the house she had moved out of and that every couple who had ever lived there had gotten divorced.

"Will you come and smudge it?" she asked.

I just about died. She knew I had been helping families since I had been talking a little bit about the spiritual side. She trusted me enough and thought I knew enough to ask me to smudge her house.

"Sure," I said.

I went and smudged her house to get rid of the bad entities. And they were bad.

I still had a strong feeling that I was supposed to be living in Shadow Crest, but I didn't know why. Not long after I'd smudged the house, Daisy, Rich's eighty-six-year-old mother who lived next door, entered the garage we shared to speak with me.

"You know, I'm psychic," she said.

I started to laugh.

"I have the gift of premonition."

I don't know if she *knew* I was supposed to live there, but I didn't have time to talk to her that day. I haven't really sat down and discussed it with her, but one day I will.

I continued to work on the case about the young woman. Everyone thought she had committed suicide when she had actually been murdered by her husband. The players continued to grow.

I also made a decision to go on another trip to see Jack in northern Arizona, something my mom had said I would do soon. We had a wonderful time together. The love and connection I felt for him was beyond this world. But it was never going to be our destiny to share our lives. He was not available to give his whole self to me, and I understood this. What I struggled with was how I was ever going to let him go, how we were going to let our relationship go.

While I was with him, I had a visitation dream, one I'd had before. Only this time it was much more pronounced. I was being attacked by a beautiful female with a dark soul. She was trying to hurt me. She wanted to destroy me. I had seen her before. Jack was at my side in the dream, giving me the strength to fight her. Just his presence was my strength, but the battle was mine.

When I woke, I kept saying, "Oh, no. Oh, no. Oh, no."

I understood at that moment that this was the female entity that had taken Mark down. She wanted to take the rest of us down, and it would have a negative impact on generations to come. I was not going to let her win. I was stronger than her. The rest of the time I was with Jack, I could not shake the encounter. It would bring me to tears just thinking about it. I knew I had to clear myself and protect myself. It was vital.

As our time together came to an end and he drove me to the airport, I could see the pain and conflict in his face. It saddened me to see him so torn between me and his life there. The choice was going to have to be made. On the surface I selfishly wanted it to be me. But deep down in my soul I knew it was time for me to move on. He had given me all he could, and now it was time to let me go, let me spread my wings and fly. Katherine had told me that I had a gift and needed to grow it and work on it. She had joked that I needed to go to Hogwarts, the witchcraft and wizardry school in *Harry Potter*. We had laughed at the time. Now in the car with Jack and silently staring out the window as we drove back to the city, I saw a sign on the side of the road that read, "Hogwarts Road, this way." It was marked with a big arrow. I knew it was God winking at me.

When I got back to the city but before I flew home, I heard back from the team that had been assembled for one of the suicide cases I was assisting. Funny how I needed to be reminded of that purpose just then. I needed to fight this bad entity that was trying to take me down. I had been given a gift from the divine.

I flew home and began packing up the ridiculously large house, trying to get rid of things I no longer needed to hold on to, including the rest of Mark's things. It was time. I didn't feel sad this time, didn't cry or have meltdowns like I had done during the last move. I had changed. I was better. I was special. Mark's death had given me a gift.

The move was difficult, exhausting, and time-consuming. I didn't have much help because everyone was busy with their own lives. My sisters helped a little on moving day, but they couldn't help me with the sadness that always enveloped me with every change. During the move I also moved Cory out of the dorms and into my duplex and then back to school again. We called it "the move that just wouldn't end."

During the chaotic move Cory and I didn't get along well and the post-traumatic stress disorder symptoms returned. I was also battling with my daughter because of her lack of help and compassion. I was feeling sorry for myself and was sliding into a place I didn't like to dwell. So I began talking to the divine/God, asking why no one ever made me their priority. Mark hadn't. My kids didn't. Jack couldn't. I was miserable and sobbing.

The answer came two days later when I was awakened in the night by a bright light in my room. I acknowledged it and turned over and went back to sleep. I awoke again a few hours later. It was early morning. I sat up in bed, still sleepy, and heard a voice. "You are not supposed to be anyone's priority right now. You have to be on your own . . . not distracted. You have work to do, and means will come to you as you need them."

And then it was gone.

In the ensuing days I reconnected with Eva and made peace with our relationship. I got Cory settled into his new place. But I struggled with my relationship with Jack. I began to feel smothered and restless, like I needed to be set free. I was constantly hurting his feelings with my distance, and I couldn't stand it. I loved him too much to hurt him. As I turned inward, I realized it was okay to be alone. I could do this now. But first I had to end my relationship with Jack, my agape, my lover. Breaking it off with him turned out to be one of the hardest things I'd ever done—maybe even harder than coping with Mark's death. It felt like a death. He was that much a part of me. But in order for me to grow, to learn, to do this divine work, I had to let him go.

Jack had helped heal my heart, and in the process he had helped save my life. He had a zest like no one I had ever met. He knew how to live in the moment and not get lost in the constant worry most people struggled with. He was an optimistic person, always focused on what he wanted, not on what he didn't want. He had taught me how to stay positive, something I had struggled with. He had also taught my kids that I would fall in love again and have relationships after Mark and that it was okay. Jack was one of my earth angels, an integral part of my journey. Maybe someday he would return to me. Only God knew.

For now I was alone . . . and ready for a new beginning.

CHAPTER 33

With each passing year since Mark's death, the kids and I have learned that you don't survive suicide but you move forward with it. His death has changed us forever. It has become a part of each of us, helping to define us as individuals.

Charlie continues to call San Francisco home. In 2011 he rode in the AIDS/LifeCycle bike ride from San Francisco to Los Angeles. He likes to get involved with anything that requires commitment and focus and makes him feel like a part of something. He still misses his dad and occasionally calls or texts me about it. His text messages often begin with *Remember when Dad used to—*

Of the three kids I think he suffered the least impact from Mark's death, no doubt because he had already moved away and was out on his own when it happened. He regrets though the fact that he had always assumed he had the rest of his life to have an adult relationship with his father. If he feels less heartache than the rest of us, he suffers just as much regret. Sometimes when I look at him, I catch my breath. It's as if I'm looking at a young Mark. He looks that much like his father. I know Mark would be proud of him and the person he has grown into. "Charlie is more of a man than I ever was," he confessed to me more than once before his death.

Eva and Ian got married on a beach in January 2012. It was a small wedding, attended by me and my two boys, Ian's parents, Mark's parents and his brother, Harry, and two friends of Eva and Ian. Eva chose a destination wedding because walking down the aisle in a big church without her dad was not an option. She didn't want his absence to take away from the joyous occasion. As it happened, it was a beautiful ceremony. I never worried they were marrying too young. They are soul mates. They complement each other perfectly. A handsome young man, Ian is six feet one inches tall, and he has dark brown hair, big brown eyes, and a big smile. His intelligence and humor give him an adorable personality. Eva calls him "a handsome nerd." He's driven to be successful and is completely devoted to Eva. He became a part of our family from day one. I often lament the fact that he never got to meet Mark, who I'm sure would have liked him.

Although Eva is happy in her marriage, she's struggling with her career. Currently employed as a project coordinator, she finds the work unrewarding. Like her father before her, she finds the corporate world toxic. She's torn between security and fulfillment. I worry that she'll never find the courage to leave if she stays too long. Once you become ensconced in the corporate world and start making money, you become stuck. Throw children into the mix, and the chances of exploring a rewarding career diminish further.

"I have to do something on my own," Eva explains. "Something I'll enjoy. But I have to get out of the corporate world, or it's going to kill me just like it did Dad. I recognize the signs. I'm unhappy, and if I've learned anything after watching Dad all those years, I need to pay attention to that."

I've tried to impress upon her that time is on her side—for now. This is her moment to create who she wants to be in the adult world. Had her father taken a leap of faith at age twenty-three or twenty-four, he'd probably still be with us.

Eva's challenge is to learn to trust her gut. She's still having vivid dreams, still tied to others through a psychic connection. My hunch is that if she pursues a career she's passionate about, those gifts will shine. She has the ability to help others. She has already helped me in my work with people like Katherine. But right now the thought of what she sees frightens her. It used to frighten me too, but it doesn't anymore. Eva has seen things since she was a little girl, when she had night terrors. But she has to get there in her own time and in her own way. I do believe that we're going to work together someday and that we're going to go into business together, helping families. That's the vision I keep getting.

Cory continues to struggle with anger, depression, and anxiety. He hit rock bottom in February when his panic attacks left him unable to get out of bed. I drove to Burlington and helped get him admitted to the hospital. There he spent forty-eight hours getting the help he had needed for years. When he was discharged, he wrapped his arms around me and said, "Thank you, Mom." It was a poignant moment for us, considering how much we had battled in recent months. He now has a strong support system at UVM and is healthier than he's been in a long time. He's registered to return to the university in the fall of 2012. At the moment he's working at a restaurant.

Lily has said that Cory will never stop grieving, and I think she's right. But as she told him during their one-on-one session, he will help others, including me with my work. We've all been touched by the dreams, the serendipity. I have the feeling it's going to be a family thing. I will never lose faith in Cory's ability to beat his illness.

Perhaps unsurprisingly, Mark's parents haven't changed a bit. They have pressured Cory to abandon his education major and help his grandfather with his little machinery business. I don't think they'll ever have the courage to let Cory be himself and lead his own life. Fortunately it's not their decision. Although they will continue to try to control Cory and others, I will encourage my children to find their own way and heal at their own pace, regardless of what their grandparents think.

For my part I continue to be open to helping others. Not long after I ended my relationship with Jack, I resumed work on the case of the supposedly suicidal young woman who had been murdered by her husband.

Not so long ago on a beautiful, balmy night, I was sitting outside and staring up at the stars. As I thought about what I'd been through recently, I began to question God, asking him if what was happening was real and if he was truly guiding me. A moment later a shooting star arced brightly overhead.

"Okay," I said, a chill running down my spine. "Okay, I get it. This is who I am. This is what I'm supposed to do."

Every time I doubt it, I get a sign.

APPENDIX

FACEBOOK NOTES

While she was in college and not long after Cory and I had moved into the apartment in Burlington, Eva set up a Facebook page for me so we could stay more connected. I started making regular posts on the page after my first one-on-one session with Lily. Mark had crossed over, and I was in desperate need of an outlet to help me express how I was feeling. The page has since allowed my friends and family to keep track of my progress . . . or lack thereof.

January 19, 2009: "Only in my dreams now"

I can only see you in my dreams now. It's not good enough, because I miss you beyond understanding. Last night we talked and hugged and laughed, just like old times. We also made peace. I will carry that dream with me forever. Forever Loved, Never Forgotten.

February 1, 2009: "They will never change"

You hope, you pray, you ignore, but the reality of the situation is, they will never change. I'm being pulled down a dark hole when I'm around them, and I can't breathe. I now know that I can't stay. It's too destructive. Part of recovery is accepting the things you cannot change. This is the toughest decision I will ever have to make, and I pray for understanding. Life will get better. It will return in all its glory. I promise!

February 12, 2009: "Challenged"

You're strong. You're brave. You can do it. Where do you find the strength to face each challenge when they come at you in multiples? Do you find the strength in those around you? Or do you dig deep inside and somehow find something left that you didn't even know you had? How do you keep giving to those you love when you find your tank is on empty? I know that I am being challenged for a reason, God. Just let me figure it out before it's too late.

February 13, 2009: "Searching"

What happened? Where did it all go? Family, friends, lake house, life. What do you do when you can't find your way back, when all that you thought was real is gone? Was it an illusion? Why does this family make it hurt so much? Why do I see them more clearly when I am looking from the outside in? When will we feel complete again? Searching—

March 12, 2009: "Why"

Over the past month I have been asking, "Why?" So many times I feel I'm going crazy trying to figure out the answer to that question. Is there a reason that bad things happen? Is there some purpose that we just don't know about? Are we supposed to get angry or just accept what's thrown at us? Where can we find answers, or do we just accept that there are none? Why? Such a big question with no answer—

May 7, 2009: "Words of wisdom"

Enjoy your present moments. Watch that sunset. Take that walk. Take good care of yourself. And be sure to see and love the people in your life. Let them know often not only with your words but also through your behavior toward them that you love and care about them. Thank you, Elizabeth Lesser.

May 22, 2009: "Memorial Day weekend"

Memorial Day, a time to remember our loved ones that have died. This weekend was a favorite of Mark's because his birthday is May 26, and he would say his birthday lasted all weekend long. We loved to watch Mark enjoy his free time. Mark loved to boat, fish, sit around the campfire, and enjoy his family on this weekend. So here is a toast to you, Mark. We miss you, love you, and wish you a happy birthday.

May 27, 2009: "Transition"

I guess transition is the place in between two places, the Limbo Land. I'm sitting here with both places I used to call home all packed up. Looking at a life that used to be. Floating in the Limbo Land and wondering what the next place will be like. I wonder if Limbo Land is sort of like the gray space. I guess that's a question for Lily.

June 11, 2009: "Pay attention"

I have to remember that there are people in this world that are only focused on themselves. Only focused on money. What would happen if those people were forced to find compassion and empathy for others? Would they be broken open and become better people? I don't know. But I do know that there are reasons people come in and out of your life. Pay attention!

July 25, 2009: "Gently guided"

It's funny how things work out . . . or don't. When faced with a tough decision, you pray and pray for an answer, when in actuality all you have to do is pay attention to the signs and you will be gently guided in a direction that totally makes sense. I have learned over the past year to pay attention to the signs. There is help all around me, and I thank God every day for that. Letting go of my life I shared with my husband is the hardest thing I will ever have to do. I, however, have all the loving memories and my amazing kids to love and hold on to. Our house may be gone, but our home is where our family is.

August 31, 2009: "Passage of time"

It's not always good to look back, to revisit the past, unless it's just to see how far you have come. A reminder of the healing that takes place through time. A personal pat on the back. You did it. You made it. You're back in life.

October 14, 2009: "The past can help"

Sometimes it takes a look through the eyes of someone else to slap you in the face and wake you up. What are you waiting for? Get out there. Create a life. I thought I was doing a good job until I realized I don't even know this new/old hometown I moved back to. What have I been waiting for?

December 24, 2009: "Life without you"

I can't believe another Christmas is upon us. The passage of time doesn't seem to dull the pain of your absence. Life just keeps going on, the joys as well as the struggles. We're better—of that I'm sure. The heart will always remember the love, honey. We grieve so deeply because we loved so deeply. Missing you beyond understanding, especially at Christmastime. Forever Loved, Never Forgotten.

April 4, 2010: "Two years"

Spring. Easter. The time of the year for rebirth, renewal, refreshing. And also the time of the year when we are reminded of death . . . and the gift of life after death. I'll spend some time revisiting Mark's death the next couple weeks. How can I not? But I will not dwell there. Instead, I will be reminded that he is walking with the Lord, happy and at peace. A place he struggled to find here. Life is a gift, and I thank God for that every day.

It's going to be my mother's time to walk with the Lord soon too, and I pray for the strength to let her go and live this life, knowing that she also will be in a much better place. Death is all around us, but life after is so incredibly amazing. Knowing this will help me through the days ahead. Forever Loved, Never Forgotten.

December 22, 2010: "Christmas without you"

Another Christmas is upon us. It's this time of the year that we are reminded of the light we carry inside us, a light that so often dims because of the stresses of life. The challenge is to keep that light bright so the stresses of life will dim. Mark is now a bright light I carry inside me. I treasure the love and know he still watches over us, helps us through the bumps, and shines in our glory. We miss you, Mark, and hold you tightly in our hearts this Christmas. Forever Loved, Never Forgotten.

April 13, 2011: "Three years ago"

I can't begin to explain the many emotions that overwhelm me on the anniversary of your death. What can I say other than I understand the struggles and demons you faced? I understand life got too hard, and I understand you loved us and we mattered. It's the understanding that's important, no matter what. It's in the understanding that you find forgiveness. I miss you beyond understanding, and I keep you close every day. For the rest of my life . . . until we meet again.

April 13, 2012: "Four years"

I guess I have the answer to the one question: How long does it take? For me it has taken four years and the love and support of my earth angels. I want to thank Mark today for this gift of insight and this undying faith his death has brought into my life. And I want to thank my earth angels. You all know who you are.

I can honestly say I'm light today. Mark is not with me. He is now on his own journey and will be there when I cross to his side one day, waiting for me with open arms on his lake in the cabin he built for us. But from now on it's my journey to finish on this earth, to use the gifts God gave me, to enjoy the love of my agape, to touch as many lives and souls as I'm capable. Forever Loved, Never Forgotten.

CPSIA information can be obtained at www.ICGtesting.com
Printed in the USA
LVOW05s0253110813

347217LV00003B/6/P